The 11+ and 13+ Handbook

A Parent's Guide to
the Selection Process for
Independent Schools in the UK

VICTORIA BARKER

Copyright © 2014 Victoria Barker

All rights reserved.

ISBN-13: 978-1495375941

ISBN-10: 1495375943

CONTENTS

Forward		1
Introduction		3

Chapter One   The 11+ and 13+ in Outline   7

i.	What are the 11+ and 13+ exams?	7
ii.	The 11+ in outline	8
iii.	The 13+ in outline	12
iv.	Scholarships	18
v.	Key tips for the 11+ and 13+ process	20

Chapter Two   Initial Research   23

i.	How do I find out about schools?	23
ii.	How do I make a shortlist of appropriate schools?	25
iii.	How important is the academic level of a school?	31
iv.	How do I assess the character and ethos of a school?	38

Chapter Three   School Visits   40

i.	Do I need to make a school visit?	40
ii.	What questions should I ask?	41
iii.	Final comments on school visits	49

Chapter Four   School Registrations   50

i.	What is oversubscription?	50
ii.	What factors determine where to register?	52
iii.	How competitive is the entry process?	58
iv.	Children with Special Educational Needs	63
v.	Tips on making your selections	64

Chapter Five   Exam Preparation   67

i.	Does my child need to prepare for the exams?	67
ii.	Should I hire a tutor?	68
iii.	How can I help prepare my child for the exams?	71
iv.	What will the 11+ exams and 13+ pretests look like?	74
v.	Can I help my child prepare for the 13+ exams?	82
vi.	Tips on exam preparation	85

Chapter Six		School Interviews	87
	i.	Should I prepare my child for the interview?	87
	ii.	How should I prepare my child for the interview?	89
	iii.	Tips for the interview	91
	iv.	What will the interviewer ask?	93
	v.	Is it OK to lie in an interview?	97
	vi.	Advice for interviews at the top independents	98
Chapter Seven		The Exams, the Offers and the Aftermath	100
	i.	How can I improve my child's exam performance?	100
	ii.	Tips for the exam for your child	102
	iii.	What happens when the final offers are made?	105
	iv.	Some final advice on final decisions	110
Chapter Eight		State School and International Applications	112
	i.	State school applicants	112
	ii.	International applicants	119
Chapter Nine		Bursary Applications	123
	i.	Should I apply for a bursary?	123
	ii.	What bursaries are available?	125
	iii.	Tips for bursary applicants	127
Chapter Ten		Resources	130
	i.	Resources for school searches	130
	ii.	Resources for exam preparation	131

Conclusion	140
Glossary	141
Secondary Qualifications in the UK	143
Websites Referenced in this Book	144
School Visit Form	145

FORWARD

The independent school sector is one of the United Kingdom's finest institutions. It includes a very large number of truly excellent schools, which contribute hugely to the good of the UK as a whole. Like many institutions in the UK, it is old and unwieldy by nature, with many a quirk. From a parent's point of view, this is one of its principle strengths: with so many schools, each with its own distinctive character and ethos, there will be a school to suit every child, if only you can find it. But it is also what makes the sector so difficult to navigate, especially on entry. For every generalisation that is made in this book, there will be exceptions: some independents do not follow the system outlined in these pages at all.

Some parents sail through the admissions process for entry into these schools with very little difficulty: they have a child who so clearly fits the profile of a particular school that the child is registered for it, sits the exams and interviews, passes with flying colours and rolls up at the school gate in September with a smile. Some parents, by contrast, experience the months or years of the 11+ and 13+ admissions process as among the worst of their lives: so much invested in it, yet so little control over its outcome! My own experience (like that of most parents, I expect) was somewhere between these two extremes. (But I still pity the parents who like me have both a boy and a girl, and are applying for single-sex schools: having just placed the first child by way of one set of admission procedures, they have to go back to square one and learn a new and different set of procedures for the second child.)

For these reasons - the system's complexity and its tendency to breed exceptions - I have set up a website as a companion to this book where the latest information can be found: www.IndependentJunction.co.uk. It is intended as a forum for parents of independent school children to share information and experience. If you find exceptions to the generalisations in these pages, if you disagree with my advice and have better to give, or if you have thoughts, suggestions, comments or questions on any aspect of the 11+ or 13+ admissions processes, please share them!

This book is a collaborative effort by a vast number of parents: I have drawn on conversations with many more friends, acquaintances and forum communicants than I can name. Thank you to each and every one of you. To those who are reading this and who have yet to discover the highs and lows of the independent school entry process: I pass on to you the proceeds of this experience with my very, very best wishes.

INTRODUCTION

Some of the best schools in the world are in the United Kingdom. Any child who enters one of the top independents in the UK is an extremely fortunate child: not only can they can expect to enjoy a happy schooling, with excellent teaching and stunning facilities, but they will have the opportunity to gain stellar results and admission into one of the world's top universities, many of which are also in the UK.

The positive results of an independent education in the UK are hard to dispute. Figures from the Independent Schools Council (ICS), which represents over 1,200 independent schools with over 500,000 pupils, show that more than half of pupils at these schools achieve A/A* grades at A-levels, compared to a national average of 27%. These pupils make up only 15% of the A-level population, but achieve one third of the top grades. These marks are earned in the more difficult subjects, furthermore, with nearly half of the top grades in the modern languages and a third in the hard sciences going to pupils from ISC schools. Success is not limited to academic results, with an astounding 38% of UK medal winners in the 2012 Olympics coming from ISC schools. (The facts and figures in the book on the independent sector's performance come from annual ISC Census (2013) and elsewhere on the ISC's website.)

These results explain why the competition for places at these schools is so fierce. For a great many of these schools, there is competition for places. Thus, a warning must be sounded from the first pages of this book: if you are new to the admissions process for independent schools, you should know that it is not easy. The process of selecting, and being selected by, an independent school in the UK can be highly labour intensive - both for the parent or guardian and for the child.* The school visits alone will take hours, not to mention the exam preparation. It is also worth knowing that the process can be stressful - especially the days spent waiting for the envelopes to arrive with acceptances or rejections. (You may hear about 'fat' and 'thin' envelopes: a fat envelope contains an acceptance, because it contains several pages of acceptance forms; a thin envelope contains a single-page 'thanks but no thanks' letter.) The admissions process can bring to light emotional and even ideological divisions within a family, whose members may have surprisingly different ideas about what is right for a child. And there are surely few households that do not experience some degree of tension over exam preparation.

* For simplicity's sake, I have referred to 'parents' throughout the text, but the reader should of course understand this to mean: 'parent or legal guardian'.

THE 11+ AND 13+ HANDBOOK

Those who are unfamiliar with the education system in the UK will be amazed at its complexities. It is perhaps safer to say that there is no consolidated system behind UK education and that the various sectors have grown up higgledy piggledy over the course of hundreds of years. The happy result of this for the independent sector is an anarchic variety, with schools to cater to many a different type of child, from the most academic to the most sociable to the most sporty. The less happy result - at least as far as this book is concerned - is that for *any* generalisation about schools in the independent sector, there will be exceptions. This book will give you an idea *in broad outline* of you are likely to encounter in the process of seeking admission to an independent school for entry at age eleven or thirteen. It will tell you *in general terms* what to expect of these schools and what they will expect of you. Having read this book, you need to go and do your own research, to discover the specific details of the admissions process of each of the schools you are interested in. Do not assume that, just because one school does one thing, others will do the same. These schools are independent in every sense.

Before moving on, I will give a word of advice on a personal level, from my own experience placing my children in schools in the extremely competitive London environment. The approach I took was very hands-on. I wanted to be sure I was doing the right thing at every step. (For those who are not confident about the whole admissions process: I write this with you in mind.) Others seemed more confident than I about their children's expected outcomes. One mother took me aside and said, 'You know, you don't have to worry. The schools will work it all out perfectly well amongst themselves.' On the evidence of the very disparate group of children in my son's prep class, her claim seems to have been true. These children all ended up in excellent schools, each right in its own way for the child who went there. I strongly suspect, however, that part of the reason for this was that these parents put a great deal of effort into ensuring the right outcome, as did their children (and probably a small army of tutors as well). It is also because the schools that they had to pick from were all excellent schools. Had they chosen different schools, these parents would probably have been equally convinced that the outcomes were the right ones.

While the Heads of the children's primary and prep schools will play an important role in steering both you and your child in the right direction for success, it is you as parent who ultimately bears the responsibility for what happens to your child. A Head's advice is no doubt invaluable, but you need to be informed as well, if only to make the job of the Head easier by being able to speak intelligently about your choices. This Head will be able to advise you all the better if you are also well-informed. Further to this, the

THE 11+ AND 13+ HANDBOOK

Head is on occasion required to put some effort into securing a place in a senior school for a child. He or she will feel more inclined to put in that effort for your child if he or she sees that you too are working towards the same end.

For anyone who is in any doubt, both 11+ and 13+ exams are extremely worthwhile for your child to sit. The Common Entrance course in particular is varied, interesting and rigorous, and the children who sit through it are extremely lucky to have done so. Both 11+ and 13+ are excellent rehearsal for the GCSE exams which children sit at age sixteen in the UK. One of the reasons that the independent schools do so well in their GCSE results is that their pupils come to them with the experience of a major set of competitive exams behind them. So, do not begrudge the amount of time that you and your child will devote to these exams. These children are learning valuable lessons: how to concentrate, how to revise, how to organise their material, how to sit exam papers, how to control their nerves. All of these lessons will stand them in good stead later on. There are more even more important lessons they are learning, too: that some things are hard, but are nevertheless worth doing properly; that hard work is the surest route to success; and that there is a great deal of enjoyment to be had in working hard and succeeding.

CHAPTER ONE
THE 11+ AND 13+ IN OUTLINE

i. What are the 11+ and 13+ exams?

The independent schools in the UK are precisely that: independent, both of the government and of each other. Like all schools in the UK, these schools are overseen by statutory bodies. However, they are free to adopt whatever admissions procedures they see fit or even to flout their own published admissions procedures, should they choose. Historically, the schools have tended to adopt broadly similar admissions procedures, which have resulted in the 11+ and 13+ nomenclature. Let me note one last time, however, that there is a danger in making any generalisations regarding the admissions procedures of schools in the independent sector. Parents must establish the specific admissions procedures of each school for which they wish to apply, *taking particular note* in the first instance of the dates on which an initial registration is required to be considered for admission. This information can be found on a school's website, so there should be no grounds for confusion.

The 11+ and the 13+ exams are different exams, taken by different children, as part of differing admissions processes - at different schools, for the most part. Children applying to schools in the independent sector usually sit *either* the 11+ or the 13+, depending on the age at which entry into their senior school is to take place, though some few children sit both. Historically, it is girls who sit the 11+ for entry into girls' senior schools (which traditionally start at Year 7), while boys sit the 13+ for entry into the boys' senior schools (which traditionally start at Year 9). Recently, however, these admissions processes have become more varied, with many schools allowing entry by way of other admissions procedures. The increasing popularity of co-educational schools has brought changes, as has the influx of international students. Many international students sit neither 11+ nor 13+ exams, but enter the school at different times and by way of more individualised admissions procedures.

Broadly, the following children sit 11+ exams for independent schools each year: girls and boys seeking admission to independent day and boarding schools that start at, or have a major intake at, age eleven. This includes children (more commonly, girls) transferring from independent preparatory ('prep') schools into independent senior schools. It also includes children transferring from state schools into the independent sector, either into senior schools or into prep schools that prepare them for the 13+ exam.

THE 11+ AND 13+ HANDBOOK

These children sit 13+ exams for independent schools every year: boys and girls seeking admission to independent day and boarding schools that start at, or have a major intake at, age thirteen. This includes children (more commonly, boys) transferring from prep schools into senior schools that use the Common Entrance exams or those that set their own exams.

Which exam will your child sit: the 11+ or the 13+? It depends on your choice of school. Some schools start in Year 7 and so have their major entry at this point, while others start at Year 9 and so have their major entry at that point. Others again have entry points in both years, so you may have a choice of two options: sitting your child for 11+ exams for entry in Year 7 or placing your child in a prep school for Years 7 and 8, so as to sit the 13+ exams for entry in Year 9. (It is unusual to gain entry into an independent school at 13+ except by way of a prep school that will 'prep' your child for the 13+ exams.)

If the school offers entry at both 11+ and 13+, you will need to decide on your point of entry in Year 5 or 6. (A child is not normally allowed to sit both 11+ exams and 13+ pretests at the same time.) In this case, the choice may come down to such issues as whether your child is ready to 'move on' at age eleven or whether he or she is late to mature academically or emotionally, and would be better prepared for exams at age thirteen. If your child is already at a prep school, the quality of this school may also influence your choice: if your child is happy at his or her prep school, you may prefer to put off the move until he or she is older.

Note that some schools also offer a 10+ entry point (either for entry into Year 6 or for deferred entry into Year 7), which may offer some children a way of avoiding the scramble at 11+. That said, the 10+ exams closely resemble the 11+ exams, so the difference is merely that the normal procedures are conducted a year earlier. The schools that do this tend to be the co-educational schools and the boy's schools with attached junior schools. Some schools use this entry point at a way to target the brightest children from the state schools, in advance of the grammar school exams at the beginning of Year 6.

ii.   The 11+ in outline

[The following needs clarification before anything else: the other two major school sectors in the UK - the 'comprehensive' and the 'grammar' schools - also have intakes at 11+. In Year 6, some children in the UK sit National Curriculum (commonly known as 'SATs') exams and proceed to comprehensive secondary schools in Year 7. Others sit exams for entry into grammar schools in those counties of the UK where these state-funded selective secondary schools still exist. Both exams are sometimes referred to as 11+, but the name is particularly used for the 11+ grammar school entry exams. The 11+ exams taken by children entering the independent schools differ from the 11+ exams taken by children entering grammar schools. Throughout this book, any reference to 'the 11+' is to be understood as a reference to the 11+ exams for independent schools.]

The 11+ exams for entry into the independent schools are the exams taken by children in the year in which they turn eleven for entry into an independent school in Year 7 in the UK system. These exams are competitive, rather than qualifying: the issue is not to show a certain level of ability but rather to show greater ability than the other children also applying to enter the same school. Parents typically register a child at several schools; some register at many. Since each school pursues its own admissions procedures, a child registered for more than one school may sit for a variety of exams, interviews and so on at different schools. As far as possible, the schools in a geographical area try to accommodate the fact that children will be sitting for more than one exam and try to avoid conflicts. In London, for instance, a number of schools have collaborated to form the North London Consortium of Girls' Schools, which facilitates the entry process by setting common exams. For the most part, however, each school operates independently.

The exams taken for 11+ admission are usually set by the schools themselves. They vary from school to school, but typically follow a fairly standard format. The Independent Schools Examinations Board (ISEB) sets papers in English, Maths and Science for use in 11+ exams, which tend to be used by co-educational schools and by girls' boarding schools. (These, somewhat confusingly, are also called Common Entrance exams, like their 13+ counterparts.) For the most part, however, the 11+ exams are set by the individual schools themselves. All schools administer the process of 11+ entry into their schools themselves.

At most independent schools, the 11+ admissions process follows a standard series of steps:

- School visits
  The process of 11+ entry starts with visits to the individual schools by prospective applicants in Year 5 and early in Year 6. These may be school open days or other individual or group visits organised by each school.

THE 11+ AND 13+ HANDBOOK

- Registration

Parents then register their interest in the schools of their choice: the schools for which their child will sit the 11+ entrance exams. The deadline for registrations is usually set in October or November of Year 6 - that is, the year preceding entry into the senior school - after which time registrations will be considered only under exceptional circumstances, such as a recent arrival from overseas. Registration for a school usually costs around £100, but it may cost more, and the fee is non-refundable once paid. The Registration Form will normally ask for your child's present school, their siblings' schools, parent's professions, previous contact with the school and the names of other schools for which you are applying. There may be a paragraph for writing about your child, in which case, the child's highest achievements and broader interests may be listed. Some schools may ask for copies of past school reports.

- References

Following registration, a reference is requested from the applicant's present school. The reference is confidential: you cannot expect to have input into it or see what it contains. These references can be quite lengthy: both the Head of the school and the applicant's form teacher will be asked to give an appraisal of the child's strengths and weaknesses, the child's academic performance to date and prediction for future academic achievement. There may be a form with set questions and also space for the Head and the teacher to give their individual assessment of the child.

- Exams

The 11+ exams normally take place in the January of Year 6 - that is, the school year preceding entry - at the senior schools themselves. They are standardly set in Mathematics and English, and it is common for a Reasoning paper to be set as well. The Reasoning in question is usually Verbal Reasoning; less commonly, a Non-verbal Reasoning paper may be added or substituted. These exams are usually roughly an hour in duration.

- Interviews

In addition to these exams, an interview takes place, again at the school, with a senior staff member or with the Head himself or herself. Sometimes parents are invited to take part in these interviews as well. Children may also be asked to attend the school for further sessions, usually a single morning or afternoon but sometimes an entire day (or overnight, in the case of a boarding school), where supervised and

THE 11+ AND 13+ HANDBOOK

informally assessed activities take place, such as sporting matches, games or even craft activities. Interviews and activity days may take place either before or after the exams.

- Results
  The 'results' of the 11+ exams are then sent out by mail to the parents in February or March of the year of entry. The marks for the exams are not given, as a rule, but parents will receive news of one of these three kinds: an outright rejection; an offer of a place at the school; or news that the child's name is on a waiting list and thus that an offer may follow. If an offer is made, an acceptance is expected fairly promptly: a date and time is given as a strict deadline for acceptance of the offer. A deposit (often, a term or a half-term's fees) is required on acceptance of a place at the school, which is non-refundable once paid.

There are variations on these procedures in some schools. One such variation has been introduced in schools where oversubscription is particularly high: a preliminary selection process or a 'pretest' which takes place in the months preceding the January exams. This pretest may take different forms: it will often consist merely of an interview or it may consist of a Reasoning test or a computerised Cognitive Ability Test - or both the interview and test. The function of the pretest is to reduce the number of children competing for places at the school, selecting those children who will then go on to sit the formal 11+ exam for entry to that school.

Other variations may be introduced by a school for scholarship applicants. At 11+, the tendency is for children to be automatically enrolled for an academic scholarship, which are offered to those who perform most impressively in the exams and interviews. There are exceptions, however: at some schools, you must state your intention, or make an application, to be considered for an academic scholarship. Some schools conduct separate exams and interviews for scholarship applicants at 11+. You should check what is involved the time of registration.

Other scholarships may also be awarded in music, art, drama and sport, on the basis of further practical tests that are conducted at the time of the interviews with the relevant Heads of Department in the school. A scholarship usually includes a reduction in fees, though this may not be substantial: many schools offer a 10% reduction only. A scholarship may come with an incentive of some other kind, however: a music scholarship may entitle its holder to free music lessons, for example. For some schools, the offer of a scholarship entitles a child to be considered (or increases the likelihood of being considered) for a bursary. When an offer is made of a

THE 11+ AND 13+ HANDBOOK

place at a school, the letter of offer will normally include any details of a scholarship or bursary that has been awarded.

iii. The 13+ in outline

The 13+ exams for entry into the independent schools are the exams taken by children in the year in which they turn thirteen for entry into an independent school in Year 9 in the UK system. To make sense of the 13+ admissions process, the first thing to note is that it is an entirely different process from the 11+ process. This distinction is particularly important because some schools have an intake at both 11+ and 13+ (predominantly, the co-educational schools) and also because some 13+ schools have junior schools attached to them (predominantly, the long-established 'public' schools). This junior school will have its own intake at 11+, with its own set of exams, which is separate from the senior school intake at 13+. For those who wish to proceed to the senior school at 13+, entry into an attached junior school at 11+ is an excellent option. Children who are accepted into the junior school often proceed without hitch into the senior school. The junior school will prepare its pupils specifically for the exams - and in particular, for the scholarship exams - of the senior school. The senior school may in turn give preference to candidates from its junior school and may even reserve places and scholarships specifically for these children.

The 13+ admissions process is generally a more protracted affair than the 11+. In most schools, the process will take several years to complete. Most children will register for several schools, though there is no necessity to register for more than one. (Indeed, you will save yourself time and effort if you enrol for one school and one only, but this course of action is usually advised only if is clearly the case that your child and the school are well-matched.) The 13+ process also admits of more variation than the 11+. Nevertheless, like the 11+, the process for all schools begins with the school visits and registration.

- School visits
  The 13+ process starts with visits to prospective schools in Years 4 and/or 5. These visits may be on open days or they may be school tours taken individually or in groups.

- Registration
  Registration for some schools takes place by the end of the year in which the child turns ten - that is, Year 5. For others, the deadline is later, in Years 6, 7 or even as late as Year 8. Some schools have a window for registrations, while others have a strict deadline, after

12

which time registration will only be accepted under exceptional circumstances, such as a recent arrival from overseas. Registration for a school usually costs around £100, but it may cost more, and the fee is non-refundable once paid. The Registration form will normally ask for your child's present school, his or her siblings' schools, parent's professions, previous contact with the school and the names of other schools for which you are registering. There may be a paragraph for writing about your child, in which case the child's highest achievements and broader interests may be listed. Some schools may ask for copies of past school reports.

- References
  All schools require a reference from the child's present school, which asks about present levels of attainment and projections for coming years. The reference is confidential: you cannot expect to have input into it or see what it contains. Like the 11+ reference, this reference may be lengthy, and require the input of both the prep school Head and form teacher.

At this point, the admissions procedures divide into differing paths: the Common Entrance path and the non-Common Entrance path. Which path your child will take will depend on the schools for which you register. Some schools use the Common Entrance exams set by the Independent Schools Examinations Board (ISEB); others set their own exams. (All these 13+ exams tend to be called Common Entrance exams, though technically the term applies only to the first of these: the Common Entrance exams set by ISEB.) A child may register for schools that use Common Entrance and also for schools that use their own exams and so pursue both paths. A school may even use different forms of exam for different applicants: Common Entrance for some and school-set exams for others. In practice, however, the two paths bifurcate during the course of Years 7 and 8:

- The non-Common Entrance path: if a child sits exams set by an independent senior school prior to the Common Entrance Exams, and then proceeds to accept an offer of a place at that school, then he or she will not need to sit Common Entrance exams;

- The Common Entrance path: if a child sits pretests for a school which uses the Common Entrance exams, and then proceeds to accept a conditional offer of a place at that school, then he or she will sit Common Entrance exams for admission to that school. (Of these schools, some also conduct scholarship exams, which a child may sit in place of Common Entrance exams.)

a. The non-Common Entrance path

At 13+, a number of children will sit entry exams set by the schools for which they have registered. The major difference between these school-set exams and the Common Entrance exams is that the former are competitive. They are like the 11+ exams in this respect. The children who do well in these exams, along with the interview and the reference from the prep school, will be more likely to receive the offer of a place at that school.

- Interviews

  In general, the interviews at 13+ tend to be more 'academic' in nature than the interviews for 11+ entry, and may involve English comprehension exercises, mental maths problems, reasoning or other IQ testing exercises, and/or spoken language testing in French or another modern European language, as well as the usual discussion of interests and aspirations. These interviews are usually conducted in the senior school by a senior member of staff or housemaster or housemistress. They usually last for 20-30 minutes, but they may last longer. These interviews usually take place in Years 6 or 7, though they may take place in Year 8, at the time of the exams.

- Exams

  Unlike Common Entrance exams, which are conducted at the prep school, school-set exams are conducted at the school themselves. These exams are usually held in January or February of Year 8. Applicants will normally receive an offer prior to March, by which time they must decide whether to accept that offer or to sit the Common Entrance exam for another school. These exams are usually set in fewer subjects than the Common Entrance: English, Mathematics, Science and sometimes also French or another modern European language. Other subjects, such as Reasoning, may also be included. The academic level of these exams will be roughly the same as the Common Entrance exams.

- Results

  For children sitting school-set exams, the results are usually posted shortly afterwards and in any case before March, when registration for Common Entrance is required. The children who accept offers at these schools no longer need to sit Common Entrance exams for school admission, but may nevertheless sit these exams along with other children in their prep schools as a way of concluding their two-year study program.

b. The Common Entrance path

The Common Entrance exams are the exams taken by the majority of applicants to independent schools at 13+. They are so-called because they are common to many of the schools conducting entrance exams at 13+. The Common Entrance exam is set by the Independent Schools Examinations Board (ISEB), an independent group of prep and senior school teachers, who also write the curriculum of the two-year program. ('Common Entrance' is also another name for the curriculum itself: the two years of study leading up to the exams.) Applicants sit these exams in a number of subjects in June of Year 8 - that is, the school year preceding entry into their senior school.

The Common Entrance exams differ from other 11+ and 13+ exams in several respects. The major difference is that the 13+ exams are taken for one school only, the right to sit the exam for that school having been established in advance by pretesting. In the two years preceding the Common Entrance exams, the range of schools for which one is seeking admission is whittled down to a single school and the Common Entrance exams are taken for entry into that school alone. The senior school sets a minimum qualifying mark for success in the Common Entrance exam, which they consider achievable by the children to whom they have made conditional offers. A second difference is that these exams normally take place at the child's prep school, which sends the papers to each child's chosen senior school to be marked. The prep school administers the process as well, registering the child for the exams and receiving the results of the exam, which it then passes on to the child and to the parents.

- Pretests
  The pretests are a competitive exam, or set of exams, that vary in form but are often set in English, Mathematics and often also in Reasoning. Some schools test Reasoning alone. Some schools use an online Cognitive Ability Test (CAT) as the basis of their pretesting. These tests include questions in Verbal, Non-verbal and Qualitative Reasoning. 'Passing' the pretest gives the applicant the ability to proceed to the next stage of the 13+ entry process: to sit the Common Entrance exam for one's school of choice.

  The aim of the pretesting is to match the school and the child, so that each child should sit these exams for a school for which they are academically well-suited. The pretests are thus competitive, rather than qualifying, and in some ways more stressful than the 13+ Common Entrance exams. In this respect, they resemble the 11+ exams and you can treat them in much the same way for the purposes of exam preparation. The pretests usually take place in Year 5 or 6, though some schools put them off until early in Year 7.

- Interviews
The interviews are an important part of the pretesting process. For some schools, interviews precede formal written exams, while for others, this order is reversed. They are similar in form to the interviews set by the non-Common Entrance schools. (See above.) These interviews usually take place in Years 6 or 7.

- The offer and acceptance of a conditional place
After pretesting and interviews, parents will be informed whether or not their child has won a conditional place at the school, subject to satisfactory performance in the Common Entrance exams. If a child is registered for more than one school, several such offers may be received. Over the course of the following months, parents must decide which offer to accept: the child sits the Common Entrance exams specifically for entry into a chosen school, the papers being sent by registered post to that school for marking.

This decision must be made by the beginning of March of the year of the Common Entrance Exams, when the prep school enrols the child's name and prospective school with the Board (ISEB) which sets the exams. In reality, the decision must be made earlier, since the schools need to finalise their list of prospective pupils and the prep schools need to know for which school each child is to sit the Common Entrance exams. Different schools require different levels of examination; the prep school needs to know the level of preparation that your child will require for his or her exams.

- Common Entrance exams
Common Entrance exams are taken in a more extended range of subjects than the school-set exams: usually English, Maths, Science, History, Geography, Religious Education, French and Latin (which is optional, but expected by the most selective schools). There are different levels of exam that can be taken in English, Maths and Latin; the senior school stipulates the level which it expects of its prospective students. The complete set of Common Entrance exams includes over a dozen exams: Maths, English, French and Latin involve more than one exam. These exams take place during one week in June of Year 8. There may be up to four exams a day, of up to 90 minutes in length.

THE 11+ AND 13+ HANDBOOK

- Final results
  The 'results' of the Common Entrance exams are typically sent through to the Head of the child's prep school by the Thursday following the exams. In practice, however, if there is a problem, the senior school will have flagged it earlier in the week.

The majority of children entering their senior schools at 13+ sit the Common Entrance exams. The process is long, so it helps to have a timeline of the various stages of this admissions process:

The 13+ Common Entrance Path

Year 4

School visits: Parents will start to visit schools on open days and school tours, to determine which schools interest them.

Year 5

Registration: The rule of thumb is that a child should be registered at their chosen schools by the end of the year in which they turn ten - that is, Year 5 - but dates vary.

Year 6

Pretests and interviews: At age ten or eleven, the child will sit pretests and interviews for the schools for which they are registered. School references will be requested.

Year 7

Conditional offers: Parents will then expect to receive an offer from one or more of the schools for which their child is registered, conditional upon their child achieving satisfactory results in the Common Entrance exams.

Year 8

Final selection: A final decision must now be taken, to determine the school for which the child will sit the Common Entrance exams. The exams are conducted in June of Year 8 and the results posted to the child's prep school the following week.

There may be variations on these procedures in some schools. The boarding houses commonly conduct a more extensive interview and activity program for selection or preselection to their schools. Applicants will be invited to the boarding house overnight, or even for the weekend, where academic exams and interviews are conducted, along with a program of team activities and events requiring the child's participation. The aim is two-fold: to give the child a taste of boarding life at the school, so that they can determine whether it is right for them, and to get a broader picture of the child's abilities. These may be conducted at any stage up to Year 8, but usually by the end of the calendar year preceding entry into Year 8. There are also variations for scholarship applicants.

iv. Scholarships

At 11+, as mentioned earlier, applicants are often automatically enrolled for a school's scholarships, which are offered to those who perform most impressively in the exams and interviews. The same is true of many of the schools that conduct their own exams at 13+. The schools that use the 13+ Common Entrance exams, however, often treat scholarship applicants separately from other students, assessing them by way of specific scholarship exams, set by the school. With respect to their scholarship applicants, then, these schools operate like other schools which conduct their own examinations, rather than the ISEB Common Entrance exams.

The 13+ scholarship exams are conducted over several days at the senior school prior to the Common Entrance exams - usually in April or May of Year 8 - with results posted some days later. Candidates sit the scholarship exams for the same school as they would otherwise sit Common Entrance. Since the scholarship exams are at a higher level than the Common Entrance exams, the results will be taken in place of Common Entrance results for all the candidates, not merely the scholarship winners. The rare exception would be a child who does not succeed in the scholarship exams and who may then be asked to sit Common Entrance exams in some or all subjects, as a means of rectifying their results.

The Scholarship exams differ from the Common Entrance exams in that they require a deeper understanding of the subject. The papers demand an ability to develop the material in ways that show individual intellectual flair. The Scholarship exams may also include a wider range of subjects: Ancient Greek may be examined, for example. There is no syllabus for these exams. The schools which prepare candidates for these exams rely heavily on past papers as an indication of what to expect. The upshot is that, if your child does not attended a prep school that specifically prepares children for the scholarship exams, he or she will be hard pressed to be able to compete in them. The children that are to sit the scholarship exams are normally selected in Year 7 and prepared in a separate scholarship set.

Thus, if you wish your child to sit scholarship exams for 13+ entry into an independent senior school, he or she will need to attend a prep school that prepares children for these exams. These are typically the larger prep schools. A prep school that is small or does not commonly send its pupils to the top independents may not be in a position to prepare your child for these exams. Even if your prep school does prepare pupils for scholarship exams, it may not prepare children for the exams of the senior school you are interested in. You will need to check well in advance that your prep school is a 'feeder school' for the senior school you are interested in.

There are other forms of scholarship besides academic scholarships. Those applying for scholarships in art, music and drama can also expect to be examined in their chosen field. Applicants for art scholarships will be expected to show an impressive portfolio of work and may also sit a practical exam. Those who apply for music scholarships will be expected to have achieved certain grades at least two instruments; the Registrar or Director of Music will be able to tell you what these grades will be, but they may be as high as a Distinction at Grade 6 for a first instrument and at least Grade 3 in a second (but note that, at some schools, scholarship applicants will be at an even higher level). A reference may be sought from the music teacher. Evidence of involvement in public performances in an established orchestra will help such an application. So too with sporting scholarships: the schools will want evidence of achievements in public competitions, beyond the A-team in the child's prep school, and may receive applications from children in national teams. Some schools also offer drama scholarships, which may be examined by both a prepared piece and by a series of improvisational exercises. Lastly, some schools offer all-round scholarships, designed to pick out children with a combination of skills or children who have demonstrated leadership potential in some way. The criteria for these scholarships are left intentionally vague, to allow schools to consider candidates on a case-by-case basis.

Some further notes about scholarships: the winner of a non-academic scholarship will need to show academic ability as well as ability in their particular field. Those selected for non-academic scholarships at 13+, for example, will need to sit Common Entrance exams or other school-set exams and to reach the stipulated levels. A further point to note is that schools will award these scholarships on any grounds they see fit. Academic scholarships, for example, may not necessarily go to those who perform most impressively in the Scholarship exams. Other factors may come into play, such as performance in interviews and performance in other fields of achievement. Lastly, note that these scholarships are generally not very lucrative. As noted of the 11+ scholarships, a 10% reduction of fees is common. Some scholarships may be up to 50%, but others again are purely nominal: it is the honour of being able to call oneself a 'scholar' or an 'exhibitioner' that is at stake. However, success in a scholarship may allow one to be considered for, or increase one's chances of obtaining, a bursary.

v. Key tips for the 11+ and 13+ process

What advice of a general kind can be given to those sitting 11+ and 13+ exams? The following suggestions apply to the entire admissions process. Advice and suggestions that are specific to the various parts of the process - selection of schools, preparation, exams and final decisions - are given in the chapters that follow.

- The single most important issue to keep abreast of in the process of 11+ and 13+ admission is the deadline for registrations. If you miss a school's deadline, you will miss the opportunity of being considered for that school. There is no general guideline as to when these deadlines are set, beyond the rule of thumb that the end of Year 5 is common for 13+ and the beginning of Year 6 is common for 11+. (Note that the registration for 13+ is commonly prior to the registration for 11+.) Registration dates vary from school to school and from year to year, so you do need to check carefully.

- Plan well in advance for every stage of the process for every school in which you may be interested: for registration, school visits and exams. Be aware, for example, that many schools have a limited number of places on school tours and that these often become booked out well in advance. It is extremely important that both you and your child attend a school tour if you wish to apply for a school, since interviewers will commonly ask a child why he or she is interested in the school and the child needs to be able to give an informed response. A school is less likely to take an interest in a child who has not made time to visit it.

- Be organised from the beginning. Make notes and keep them in a book or folder. Researching schools takes a large amount of time and you do not want to be repeatedly returning to a school's website, trying to track down information that has been mislaid. With so many schools, each with different entry procedures, it is very easy to become confused.

- It is very important to establish exactly what is required at each step of the application process in terms of preparation. Make sure you know what is involved and prepare your child for each and every step of the process. Take every step seriously; do not assume that any step is a mere formality. Do not assume that your child's entry is assured until such time as you have received a formal offer in writing and paid the final deposit towards the first term's fees.

THE 11+ AND 13+ HANDBOOK

- Think out in advance what you want to achieve at each step of the admissions process. Make advance notes for a school visit, for example. You will not remember everything that you want to ask unless you do. (There is a form on the Independent Junction website that you can use for the notes for school visits.)

- Try not badger the Registrar or Admissions Staff of the schools with questions; they are undoubtedly overworked. Try to obtain the information from another source first. If some aspect of the process is unclear to you, however, and you cannot find the answer on the website or in the information booklets the school provides, contact the staff to clarify what you want to know.

- Whenever you attend an interview, pretest, exam or even just a school visit, make sure that your child appears neat and well-presented. It will make a good impression; it will show that you care enough to put in the effort. It is best to wear a school uniform on all such occasions, even if it is not requested and even if it is on the weekend. The Admissions Staff and the teachers who interview your child have to imagine him or her as a pupil at the school: wearing a uniform will help. If your present school does not have a uniform or your child is home schooled, wear clothes that are generic and understated and perhaps even a little uniform-like. Under no circumstances have your child appear in the uniform of the school for which you have applied until such time as he or she has been formally admitted into it. (It has been known to happen.) Your child should also wear any badges (form captain, house captain, etc.) that they may have earned from their present school, especially to an interview. Wearing these will make your child more confident and give them something to talk about.

- Remember that these schools are about relationships. Even at the earliest stage of proceedings - open days and school visits - both you and your child will do well to express your interest in your chosen schools, so that the staff at these school will be inclined towards you. You may wish to remind your child that you expect them to be polite, friendly and respectful in any interaction with any staff member at these schools (or you may simply take it as understood).

- Where you believe a school to be perfect for your child - and especially if there is no other that so closely fits your child's profile - you may wish to communicate this opinion to the school's Registrar or Head. The school will feel a greater commitment to you if they know you are committed to the school. You can signal this commitment in a number

THE 11+ AND 13+ HANDBOOK

of ways. You can tell the Registrar or Head yourself, if you have the opportunity. You or your child can communicate this in the formal interview. You can tell the Head of your present school, in the hope that he or she will share this opinion and pass it on in the reference. Another option (not advised at 11+, but a serious option at 13+) is simply to register for that school and no other. The schools typically ask whether you are registering for others; if you are not, it communicates a clear intent.

There is one aspect of the admissions process which will not receive attention in the pages that follow, but which nevertheless deserve thought: the references that your present school sends on to the senior schools for which you register. These are not discussed in detail, because they do not involve you: they are confidential references sent from one Head of School to another. Nevertheless, the following points are worth noting:

- You are not the only one working towards your child's admission into your chosen school: your child's teacher and Head will also do their bit. You should keep them fully informed of the decisions you make about prospective schools. At the very least, let them know that you appreciate the time and effort they will put in to preparing your child for the exams and interviews and writing references. At all times, be courteous to and respectful of those in your present school who are helping you with this admissions process.

- It is probably best not to rely on the form teacher or Head to remember your child's achievements - even those within the school - when writing your child's reference. Help them with the information they need. You cannot tell them what to put into the reference, but you can help them by writing a detailed CV, listing your child's achievements, both within the school and without. Give copies to both teacher and Head. You are not normally invited to attach a CV to your application, but you nevertheless want that information conveyed to the senior school in one way or another.

- You might also like to suggest best behaviour to your child in the months leading up to the time when your teacher and Head will be writing the reference and making recommendations to senior school Heads and Registrars. It stands to reason that the most recent impressions that your child has made will be front of mind when that teacher is invited to give his or her impressions of your child's potential.

CHAPTER TWO
INITIAL RESEARCH

i. How do I find out about schools?

The process of finding out about schools and applying to them can be arduous. Part of the problem is that there are simply so many schools. Another is that they all appear to make exactly the same claims: to put the child first, to make the most of their potential, to nurture and to challenge them, etc., etc. And, while you can glean a huge amount of information from the schools' websites, you cannot obtain the very piece of information you actually want: what is the school actually like? Will it suit my child? Will my child be happy there?

If you are in the initial stages of researching prospective schools for your child, the best advice may be this: gather information on schools from *every* source available, without putting too much weight on any single source. Start trawling through websites; talk to teachers, Heads and other parents; keep an eye on internet forums. In the early stages of your research, however, do not put too much store by any single piece of advice given to you about a particular school. You need to find out for yourself. For many parents, this will be their first experience of feeling that their child's future lies in the hands of others. In this situation, it is easy to be misled by other people's opinions. Take others' advice 'on notice' - whoever they may be, however authoritative or well-meaning. You may be misled by the Head of your child's present school just as easily as by your neighbour. When someone tells you that a school is good, bad or indifferent, remember that their criteria in making this assessment may be directly opposed to your own. It is also worth noting that advice does not become more valuable simply because you have paid for it.

These are some of the places you can go for information about schools that may be right for your child. (Websites mentioned are listed at the back of the book and links can be found on the Independent Junction website):

- The websites of the schools
  You will be able to learn a great deal about a school from its website: its curriculum, leaver's grades and university destinations, admissions procedure, fees, and so on. Usually there is a message from the Head which explains what he or she thinks is distinctive about the school and describes his or her vision for it, plans for development and so on.

THE 11+ AND 13+ HANDBOOK

- Further information given out by the schools
  A school's prospectus, school magazines, student magazines and so on are a mine of information. The prospectus does not usually add much beyond what is on the website. The magazines, however, will tell you a great deal about the activities the pupils are taking part in: sporting matches, school trips, clubs, concerts, plays, art exhibitions and so on. The school will give you a pack of further materials at an open day or you can ring and ask them to send it to you.

- The school's open day
  School visits are discussed at length in Chapter Three, below.

- School reports
  A school's report, available from the website of the relevant inspecting body (which in England will be the Independent Schools Inspectorate), provides a wealth of information on all aspects of the school's provision of education and care.

- Websites of the various independent schools bodies
  The most useful of these are the Independent Schools Council (ISC), the Scottish Council of Independent Schools (SCIS) and the Headmasters and Headmistresses Conference (HMC).

- Your child's present school
  Ask around at your school for information and advice about the school that interests you. The school may be able to put you in contact with former parents whose children attend this school.

- Independent publications
  The Good Schools Guide is the best known of these. It has listings on over 1000 schools from all educational sectors in the UK, which claim to be unbiased and fair. The school that interests you may or may not be listed (and there are surely many 'good schools' which are not). *Tatler* also publishes a *Schools Guide* which evaluates the leading independent senior schools. *The Metropolis Guide to Boarding Schools in the UK* is fairly comprehensive, giving a page-long introduction to each boarding school.

- Independent websites
  There are a number of independent companies with websites where you can conduct school searches: the website of *The Good Schools Guide*, the Independent Schools of the British Isles (ibsi), best-schools.co.uk

24

and UK Boarding Schools all provide directories which you can search using a range of different criteria.

- School expos
  A large exhibition is staged in London and various centres overseas every year called the 'Independent Schools Show'. Many schools set up booths and have staff members on hand, including sometimes the Head and the Registrars themselves. There is also a program of speakers on a wide range of topics concerning independent education. The boarding schools in particular have a strong presence at this show. (Some of the most selective schools are already so oversubscribed that they tend not to promote themselves in this way.)

- Private consultancies
  There are a number of companies that will advise you on the schools that best fit your criteria. If you do not have time to do the research yourself, or are simply befuddled, these may be for you. You should have no trouble locating them via a web search. They tend to be expensive, but not nearly as expensive as the costs you will incur if you make the wrong decision about which school is most appropriate for your child. Be careful about what you are subscribing to, if you give them your details. You may feel it is not in your best interests for these consultancies to approach the schools on your behalf, for example.

- Forums
  If you wish to post questions, Mumsnet.com has a general secondary schools forum, and elevenplusexams.co.uk has a forum intended for grammar school parents where independent school parents nevertheless meet. The Independent Junction website has a forum set up specifically for independent school parents.

ii. How do I make a shortlist of appropriate schools?

If you are looking for an independent senior school in the UK, the first place to look is in the mirror, as it were. Start by considering what is important to you in your child's schooling. The first task is to set the parameters of what is possible for your child's schooling: practically, financially, emotionally, academically and in other ways that are particular to you. At the earliest stages of this process, you should consider the entire family context and the interests of all its members. Every family member has a stake in the decision, even though it centres on the one child. For example, the decisions you make for the older child will have consequences for the younger: try to identify what these might be. If there are disagreements within the family as to what sort of school is right for your child, these should be brought to light early in the admissions process, so that they are open for discussion. For all families, it is probably best to devote time to an open discussion of these issues, rather than assume that everyone is on the same wavelength.

If you conduct a web search of independent schools in the UK, you will soon find yourself being overwhelmed with choice. Besides selecting by region, you will need to use whatever criteria you can to narrow down the number of schools of interest to you. Beyond the geographical, the most obvious differences between the schools will be: some are boarding and some are day schools (while some are both); some are co-educational and some are single-sex schools; some offer A-levels and some offer the International Baccalaureate. These, then, may be the first decisions you make. How you address these issues will be influenced by the specific makeup of your family and your own situation as parents: the availability of time, finance, desire for involvement in the school and so on. If you have more than one child, however, you must first address the question of whether these children will go to the one school or to different schools:

- There may be purely practical reasons for preferring the one school for all your children, such as ease of travelling to and from school. Remember that (irritatingly) term times vary among schools, so that a two-week holiday period commonly spins out to three weeks or more when your children attend different schools. This can be a very serious issue for working parents. A commitment to the one school will also minimise the demands on you in terms of your attendance at concerts, speech days, parent evenings and so on. If a school has a policy of giving preference to siblings, this is worth bearing in mind. There may also be deeper advantages to being a 'single school family', in that family bonds are built by way of shared experiences of schooling.

- Against this, the following question must be weighed: will all your children thrive in the same environment or will they do better at schools that are tailored to their particular natures and educational needs? It is not unusual to have children in the one family whose academic, sporting and creative skills are markedly different, or whose psychological and emotional needs likewise differ. It may do the younger children a great disservice to try to fit them into the mould created by the first. In short, the single-school policy limits your choices - especially if you have both a boy and a girl and so must choose a co-educational school.

a. Boarding or day school?

For many parents, a boarding school is not merely the best option, but the only viable option. By senior school, the school work has gone beyond the point where most parents can make a useful contribution; younger children have a prior claim on their parent's time; the parents may be too tired after their working day to give the help needed. In any case, the school best suited to their child may be so distant that the commute is not viable. Add to these considerations, the benefits that a boarding school can provide in terms of physical and social environments, and the decision for these parents is straightforward.

For others, the best course of action is not evident. For tightly-knit families, the loss of a child for weeks at a time is a pain that none of its members wish to bear. Shy children, solitary children who are content in their own company, and children who for whatever reason have a particular love of their home life may all find the hubbub of boarding house life intolerable. Where both boarding and day schools are options, and there are considerations for and against each, the choice can be a difficult one.

The best advice that can be given to any parent struggling with the question of boarding versus day schools is to explore the options at first hand. Any discussion of the benefits of a boarding school, pursued in the abstract, amounts to very little when compared to visiting a boarding school and looking at what the children do on a day-to-day level in their school and in their houses. Many parents who would never have considered a boarding school are won over by what they see if they chance to visit one. For those at the early stages of this process, here are some of the general considerations that bear on the choice of boarding versus day, prior to questions about specific schools:

- Considerations in favour of a boarding school
  The strongest arguments for a boarding school are the time and space it provides its pupils. With the school's facilities all on site, much of child's normal daily hassle is removed. The time otherwise wasted in traffic or trains is freed up for more worthwhile activities. Space is provided by the superb environments in which these boarding houses are set: acres of land, with gardens, vegetable patches, ponds, streams, playing fields, farms and so on are common. For many boarding children, a tranquil setting, free from the distractions of urban life, is a major factor in their success at school. Add to this a ready set of like-minded companions, with whom to share a vast array of activities and interests. Add, lastly, qualified staff at hand to provide support for the

child's school work. Because both teachers and pupils are together on site, solid relationships form, which in turn contribute to the pupil's success.

Boarding schools are not what they once were. Children are no longer obliged to go for weeks on end without seeing their parents. Parental involvement is encouraged wherever possible; parents attend sports events, concerts, social events and so on, just as they would in a day school. There is now much greater flexibility in boarding arrangements: full boarding, weekly boarding or flexi-boarding are all possibilities. The influx of international children, who come with high expectations of their standards of living, has brought about a steady improvement in the facilities within the houses themselves, all for the better.

The Heads of the boarding houses report that the concern most commonly expressed by prospective parents is that their relationships with their children will suffer. In fact the opposite is the case, according to these Heads: boarding means that the time a parent spends with his or her child is 'quality' time, free from the pressure of school routine and arguments about homework. In the boarding houses, homework is merely part of the routine of daily life. So too with the other aspects of boarding life: a child will 'muck in' and give things a go in a boarding house, with the encouragement of teachers and friends. Thus children learn independence in a structured, safe environment and emerge from their boarding schools with confidence and maturity.

- Considerations in favour of a day school
Any independent school Head will tell you that, no matter how much a school contributes to the success of a child, the greater contribution to their success will have been made by the child's parents. There is no-one who cares about the success of your child as much as you do, and no-one watching as closely as you are, to make sure that he or she is happy and flourishing. Many parents feel that they have lost sight of their responsibility towards a child if they are leaving those day-to-day assessments to someone else. If you are a parent contemplating boarding school, ask yourself how you might feel if your child were inadvertently to refer to their boarding school as 'home'. When a child is spending the greater part of their life at boarding school, it is natural that it should come to figure as such.

It may be, however, that you can keep both options in play and pursue each as circumstances demand. Many schools are both boarding and day, allowing children to switch between the two. If you are considering boarding at a later stage or if other siblings must also be considered, it may be best to have the flexibility such a school can offer. Furthermore, in such schools, the benefits of boarding are also enjoyed by day pupils. Such schools are typically modelled on the 'house' system, giving children a house (or at the least, a set of rooms) to return to during breaks and free time. These houses have housemasters or housemistresses, who are on hand to ensure the pupils' well-being.

b. Co-educational or single sex school?

The best argument for each of these styles of education is the excellent schools they have produced: there are flourishing schools across the UK of each type. Some of the best schools in the UK are single sex, so they will naturally be preferred by many parents. Indeed, for many parents the issue will not be an ideological one at all. They may have a preference for a certain school on other grounds and whether it happens to be co-educational or single sex is a secondary issue. For those who do wish to consider the issue in the abstract, these are the outlines of an argument each way:

- Considerations in favour of co-education
  Many parents see segregated schools as an outmoded relic of former days, which are happily receding into the past. Increasing numbers of parents are opting for co-educational schools because they offer an environment in which boys and girls come to know each other as people, rather than as members of the opposite sex. There are immense benefits to co-educational schools: they provide for a healthy, well-balanced social setting in which the talents of all can be celebrated. Thus, the talents traditionally proper to the one sex can be pursued precisely because they are beneficial to the other: lessons in confidence and self-assertion are traded with lessons in diligence and organisation. It is also worth mentioning that some of the UK's top co-educational schools now give girls access to the superb facilities and the prestige that were once the preserve of the all-boy public schools. That in itself is enough to convince many parents of girls of the merits of co-education.

- Considerations in favour of single-sex schools
  It is a commonplace that boys mature later than girls and it is widely held that they need specific educational input to see them through the

process of attaining social and moral maturity. The media has in recent years run a series of alarmist reports about how boys are likely to be put off doing well in academic arena where they perceive that they are being outshone by girls. What is needed to reverse the trend of receding motivation is an environment where boys can flourish without being self-conscious about their perceived roles in relation to the other sex. Such worries are best put off until the boy is old enough to deal with them in a mature manner.

Meanwhile, the arguments in favour of girls' schools are clearly borne out by statistics. On their website, the Girls' Schools Association points to research by the Institute of Physics showing that girls at independent girls' schools are 1.5 times more likely to study Physics at A-level than girls at independent co-educational schools. If the presence of boys means that girls are being put off studying hard sciences at these higher levels of schooling, you may rightly wonder about the broader impact on your daughter's education of boys in the classroom. Educators point out that there is a fundamental difference between making a subject available in the curriculum and encouraging a child to take it. The independent girl's schools are particularly good at encouraging high aspirations in their girls, on the assumption that every subject is a 'girl's subject'.

Attending a single-sex school does not mean that your child will be isolated from members of the opposite sex. Many boys' and girls' schools forge links with each other, sharing musical, artistic and social activities. Nevertheless, the numbers of co-educational schools is on the rise in the UK, mainly because many single-sex schools have started admitting members of the opposite sex. This is particularly true in the later senior school years. A number of schools now offer single sex teaching until Year 11 and a co-educational Sixth Form in Years 12 and 13. The children in these schools may benefit from the best of both worlds, as it were. Note, however, that in such schools, the ratio of the sexes may not be 50:50, unlike in the established co-educational sector.

c. A-levels or International Baccalaureate?

The majority of UK parents simply assume that their child will pass through the UK education system and so emerge with a set of A-level public examinations results at the end. For many parents, there is no need to question this assumption: the A-levels are offered by almost every UK independent school and provide the standard qualification for entry to tertiary institutions across the UK. Parents may like to be aware, however, that they have a further option, in the form of the International Baccalaureate (IB). Many schools in the UK offer the IB Diploma to their pupils and, for many talented children, it offers a breadth and independence of study beyond that available to A-level students. What is more, some of the best-ranked IB schools in the world are in the UK. This is why IB students are increasingly being accepted by the best universities not only in the UK but across the world. For international children, or children whose tertiary education may not lie in the UK, the IB Diploma may offer a good alternative qualification.

In most cases, this decision can be put off until later years, when it will be influenced by your child's intentions for university study. It is nevertheless important to be aware at this stage that the alternative exists, because it may inform your choice of school: some schools offer the IB alongside A-levels, while others prefer it to A-levels. The webpages of the International Baccalaureate Organisation provide details of the IB Diploma and the schools that offer it.

iii. How important is the academic level of a school?

Assuming you have come this far, the next questions you will want to ask are probably even more difficult: how academic is my child and how academic should his or her school be? For some parents, the answer to these questions will be evident: if your child is highly academic, you will want his or her school to be as academic as it can be. The parents of these children will often simply apply to the schools that top the academic league tables and leave the rest to sort itself out. If your child is highly academic, you are lucky on many counts, not least the fact that there are some very academic schools in the UK. If you and your child are prepared to do the work necessary to be selected for them, your child may attend one of the best schools in the world. These schools are not, by the way, the 'hot-houses' described in some sections of the media. They are truly excellent schools that foster the intellectual and emotional lives of their pupils in every way possible.

Many a parent desires nothing more than that his or her child should gain admission to one of these highly academic schools. However, given that they are populated by the seriously academic - pupils who put in hours of homework for no better reason than they enjoy it - you may wish to question whether you really want your child to attend such a school if he or she does not fit the profile. Even if he or she were to gain entry, there is no fun to be had languishing in the bottom set of such a school, feeling like the village idiot. Do not be under any misapprehension about the standards expected at these schools: in some, a large percentage of pupils will get an A* in every subject they sit at GCSE, a feat which requires real commitment. Such a school does not look on a 'B' in a public exam with any measure of sympathy. Some schools have many years of unbroken records of A/A* grades in some subjects. Imagine being the child who fears that he or she might break that record.

There is a further issue to bear in mind here, which will not appear pressing to parents of children at age eleven or thirteen, but which will become increasingly apparent as the A-levels approach. When it comes to university admissions, the pupils in the most selective schools are competing against each other for admission to the top universities - and this can be a most unpleasant experience for a child who is not as accomplished as his or her friends. The schools on the top of the leagues tables have selected their cohort all along for their potential as Oxbridge candidates. In some schools, more than 90% of students will apply to Oxbridge and each of them will have the marks and the ability to succeed there. However, these universities cannot admit the vast majority of a single school. It is widely held that Oxbridge is presently admitting the upper limit of the numbers that can reasonably be taken from any single school. This leads to the apparently paradoxical situation that a child may be less likely to win an Oxbridge offer if he or she is applying from one of the most selective schools, as against one of the less selective.

There are various effects of this: a highly selective school will know that it can do little to improve its Oxbridge numbers, so it may provide less help to its Oxbridge applicants than schools that are eager to improve their Oxbridge numbers. Indeed, knowing that each Oxbridge college will only take one child from that school at most in a given field, the school may not support more than one such application. But whose application will it be? The school is not itself entitled to make the decision, so the children in effect have to work it out among themselves. Naturally, the most accomplished pupils will have earned the right to their first choices. The experience can, once again, be most demoralising for the child at the bottom of the school, who is left with the scraps after everyone else's preferences have been declared. And this is even though this child will likely attain an A average. The child's problem is simply that most others in the school will attain A*.

These are considerations to bear in mind as you consider the academic level of the schools in which you are interested. Perhaps surprisingly, the schools with the highest numbers of Oxbridge acceptances in the UK may also be the schools with the highest numbers of Oxbridge *rejections*, since such a huge percentage of their pupils will make these applications. If your aim is Oxbridge, and you have doubts about how your child might fare in one of the very academic schools in the UK, you should be aware of this issue. The point is that it is not evident that every child should simply go to the most academic school available to them. The ideal is in fact that a child would sit somewhere in the middle of the range of academic ability of pupils at their senior school. That way, the more able would stimulate the child to reach a higher academic level, while he or she will not suffer the loss of self-esteem that comes from being at the bottom. While obviously unrealisable for everybody, this ideal may be realisable for you. You should try, therefore, to establish as best as possible the academic level of your child and the academic level of the schools that interest you. Once you are confident that you know these, then you can try to match the two as best you can.

a. How do I assess my child's academic level?

As far as academic standards are concerned, you must do your best to assess the academic potential of your child - being as candid with yourself as optimism allows. The academic potential of a ten-year-old is often surprisingly difficult to ascertain, even by those who know the child best. However, there are ramifications for aiming either too low or too high in determining which schools may be available to you, so you need to do it. Aim too low and you rule out excellent schools that would gladly open their doors to your child. Aim too high and you may find the admissions process a very depressing experience indeed. Worse, your child's sense of failure may undermine his or her confidence for years to come. A reasonable assessment of your child's potential is crucial, so that you do not waste time, money and effort on schools that are not suitable. How do you make such an assessment?

- National Curriculum assessments
  If your child is in a state school and working towards the 11+, their National Curriculum teacher assessments (or SATs) will tell you whether he or she is on track to reach Level 5, which is the level the independent schools generally require at 11+. (That said, you should note that many of the more difficult questions in the 11+ exams are at the absolute upper limit of difficulty at this level.) Find out from your child's form teacher what his or her level is and what it is projected to be at the end of Key Stage Two - that is, by the end of Year 6. All primary schools are required to make these assessments and there should be no problem obtaining them. You can then use this

THE 11+ AND 13+ HANDBOOK

information to discuss with a prospective school whether your child is at the level they expect. The Registrars of the schools which take primary school children at 11+ will be familiar with the National Curriculum assessment levels and what they mean.

- Internal school assessments

  Independent schools do not standardly conduct SATs assessments, but will have their own assessment procedures. If your child is already at an independent school, talk to the teachers about how your child is performing in these assessments. Ask about your child's academic ability relative to the class as a whole. Be wary of this information: clearly, your child's position in the class is primarily an indication of the ability of the class as a whole, rather than that of your child. So you also need to know whether the cohort as a whole is strong or weak. If your child attends a large prep school with a varied cohort, then your child's ranking will provide useful information. As far as 13+ entry is concerned, the school will be aware of the marks stipulated for entry by each school. From Year 5 onwards, a prep school will be starting to match its cohort to the senior schools, using this range of stipulated marks to guide them. Ask the teachers or the Head about the marks stipulated by the different schools and find out what where in this spread your prep school is anticipating your child will sit.

- CAT tests

  One further piece of information that prep schools often use as a guide in making assessments of a child's potential is the results of any CAT tests the school has conducted. The most recent version of these tests show the relative strength of a child in four areas of reasoning: Verbal, Non-verbal, Qualitative and Spatial. These marks are used by schools as a guide to projected marks in the GCSE exams. The school may share the results of these tests with parents, so as to help guide them towards a school at the right academic level for the child. The average score for these tests is 100; the most academically selective schools will be looking for a CAT test score of 120 or higher, as least in the Verbal and Qualitative Reasoning tests, since such a score correlates highly with the attainment of A/A* grades in GCSE.

- Specimen Exam Papers

  If you are still feeling unsure - or you are not confident of your present school's assessment of your child - another indicator that you can use is the specimen examination papers for 11+ or 13+ entry, many of which are made available by the schools on their websites. (See the Independent Junction website for a list and links to these.) Some of these include marking schemes. The schemes are easier to follow for Mathematics and Verbal Reasoning than for English, but you should be able to get some idea of a rough grade, even in English. The marks your child obtains in these specimen papers may then be used as a measure to assess your child's suitability for prospective schools.

If you are using these specimen exams not merely as exam preparation, but also to assess your child's potential, you should note the following: if a child does intensive exam preparation, their final mark many improve by as much as 10-20% from the mark they were getting prior to the preparation. Thus, your assessment of your child's academic potential should include an assessment of his or her ability to prepare for these exams. If your child is clever, but is unwilling or unable to spend time preparing for the exams, then he or she may not perform as well as another child of lesser ability who is well-prepared. Inversely, if your child does averagely well at school, but is prepared to devote six months or so of solid work leading up to the exams, then you can apply for schools further up the academic scale, as it were. The schools argue that they are looking for academic 'potential', but a large part of this potential is, obviously, the will to learn and to succeed in exams. But note also what the Heads warn about 'inflated scores' at 11+: if your child enters a school on marks that are 'inflated' by intensive preparation, the child will be under constant pressure to maintain these high grades throughout their senior schooling.

b. How do I assess a school's academic level?

How can a parent establish the academic level of a school? The schools themselves typically publish their performance data for GCSE and A-levels exams on their websites or in the brochures given out to prospective parents. This information will normally include a list of the leavers' grades and university destinations. It may also include information about a school's ranking on one or other of the leagues tables. The following are the indicators that you can use to assess a school's academic performance:

- The leavers' grades
  This raw data is probably the most useful information available to you. If you already have an idea of the types of subject your child may be likely to study at GCSE and A-levels, look at the percentage of A/A* grades achieved in these subjects. Obviously, the more the better. You can probably discount the odd anomaly of a child who underperforms. However, if you are aiming high for your child, you will want to know that there is a substantial cohort who are so well-supported by the school that they achieve the highest grades.

THE 11+ AND 13+ HANDBOOK

- University admissions

The other significant information is the destination of the pupils leaving the school. The schools should provide lists of the leavers' university destinations for the past few years. The statistic that will stand out is the number of Oxbridge placements. It is simply not the case, however, that Oxbridge is the best destination for all subjects. You will also want to see the names of colleges of other Russell Group universities on the list. (See the Russell Group website for what these are.) The best school in some subjects may not even be among the well-known universities, however. Unless you are very familiar with the tertiary sector, it will be difficult to know what constitutes a successful university placement. You will probably need to speak to the staff member in charge of university admissions to make sense of the list. The schools should be enthusiastic about giving this advice. The questions to ask here are: how many of your school leavers gain admission to a Russell group university? Is there a good range of areas of study represented?

Another way of approaching the school's list of university destinations is to ask about the percentage of pupils who receive their first choice of university place. However, once again, this information cannot be taken at face value. To interpret the answer, you will also need to know whether the pupils are encouraged to be ambitious in their university applications or whether the school prefers to guide their pupils towards universities where they can be confident of success. If the school is doing well, it will be encouraging its pupils to make ambitious university applications - many of which will be to Oxbridge or to Russell group universities. This may lower the percentage of pupils who achieve their first choice of destination.

- League tables

The most common way of assessing schools' performance, relative to each other, is by the league tables. The league tables are compiled by information derived from two major public examination processes in the UK: GCSE and A-levels. Various newspapers publish these league tables, around the end of the calendar year, using information supplied by the Department of Education of results from the preceding school year. Most well-known are the tables published by *The Telegraph* and *The Sunday Times*, which are based on the information provided by the Department of Education or the Independent Schools Council. These tabulate the percentage of A/A* grades achieved at A-level, as a percentage of entries.

THE 11+ AND 13+ HANDBOOK

The BBC also publishes a leagues table, based on a points system allocated for each mark at A-levels. Another league table is available on best-schools.co.uk, based on information supplied directly by the schools themselves. This is an advantage, because many schools either do not report their results to the Department of Education and so are not included on the league tables, or use qualifications not included in the Department of Education data. However, the best-schools table is limited in a different respect, in that it only includes the top 100 schools. The one thing you will notice is that a school will often be ranked differently on the different tables (and this is aside from the schools that may be missing entirely). This in itself should warn against taking any of the tables as definitive. However, you may be able to get some broad idea of where a school stands, as against others, from these tables. (For more on the leagues tables, see Chapter Four.) You can also ask a school to explain its league table rankings to you.

One last consideration bears on the question of the academic level of the school: culling. In order to make sense of A-level results, you need to know whether the school culls students who do not achieve A/A* grades at GCSE, so as to improve its results on the league tables. Once again, GCSE may seem a long way away, but it should figure in your consideration of schools at both 11+ and 13+. Culling is a big issue at some independent schools: it occurs even in lower years in some schools, so you ought to be aware of it. It may or may not concern you, depending on what sort of results you expect your child to attain. For some children, the idea that they will lose their place at the school if they get a B or two will certainly be an incentive to do well. For others, the teenage years will be hard enough without adding that additional stress.

The question of a school's academic level is directly linked to questions of the level of competitiveness of entry into that school. (This topic will be discussed in greater detail in Chapter Four.) Broadly speaking, the more academic the school, the higher the grades the school will expect of its applicants in its entrance exams. After all, the school's academic level will in part be determined by the level of selectivity it adopts in its admission procedures. However, you should note that the two are not directly correlated: there are other issues which affect competitiveness, such as prestige, facilities and the availability of other schools in the area. While it is true that the more academic schools are more selective, the inverse is not true: simply because a school is difficult to get into does not mean that it is more academic. If you are looking for a highly academic school, you should look at the school itself, its character and stated priorities, not at the competitiveness of its entry processes.

iv. How do I assess the character and ethos of a school?

There are many schools in the UK with excellent records of achievement, excellent facilities and so on. What distinguishes these schools, one from the other, has more to do with the values and attitudes that the staff and pupils of the school share: its ethos. The ethos of a school is not something that you will be able easily to discover from the school's website or prospectus. It cannot easily be described. To learn more about it, you will need to talk to people, since it is in large measure the people who create a school's character. Ideally, the distinctive ethos of the school will be what unites the Head, teachers and pupils with a sense of common purpose. Assessing a school's atmosphere and character is crucially important in making a decision about whether it will be right for your child. You need this assessment, so as to judge whether the school promotes values that you and your child will be comfortable with. You need this assessment to decide whether your child will fit into the school, whether your child will feel they belong and hence whether or not they will be happy there.

The best way to gauge the atmosphere and character of a school is by visiting it. These are some of the people you may wish to speak to, if you can:

-   The Head
    In a large public school, it may not be possible to speak to the Head in person. The demands on a Head's time in running such a large community - and sitting on other committees and bodies - are substantial. In a small school, however, the Head will usually try to make himself or herself available to speak to prospective parents. This is as it should be. In a smaller school, the influence of the Head may be substantial. The effects of his or her leadership style will ripple across the entire school population. You may wish to ask the Head what he or she thinks are the most significant characteristics of the school and its pupils.

-   The teachers
    On open days and school visits, it should be possible to speak to a large number of teachers and form an opinion of their attitudes and motivations. Principally, of course, you are interested in their manner towards the pupils. The key to a happy school is that its pupils should feel that the teachers actually care about their progress. The purpose of speaking to the teachers is less to find out about the curriculum, class sizes and so on, but rather to determine whether they show an interest in and concern for their pupils.

- The pupils
On open days, it will probably be a pupil who takes you on a tour of the school. This is an excellent opportunity to find out about what the pupils think of their school. In the next chapter are some of the questions you might direct to a pupil guide. The point is, once again, to forgo asking questions that can be answered with a trip to the website, but rather to ask about the nature of the pupils' relationships with their teachers and with each other. You should be able to gauge whether the pupil is proud of their school, even by such small cues as the way they wear their uniform. Pride is difficult to simulate: you should be able to identify it when you see it.

- Other parents
The parents of children who are already at the school are the best source of information that you have about the atmosphere and character of a school. You must of course be wary of others' opinions, in that their criteria for judging a school may well be different from your own. This should come as no surprise and it's something you can work around by simply asking further questions which reveal what their criteria are. Other parents are nevertheless your best source of information for the simple reason that their perspective is the same as yours: it is the perspective of a parent. Seek out other parents for what they can tell you about the schools you are interested in. If you cannot find them through friends or acquaintances, seek them out on forums. Don't be shy: parents are usually keen to share their experiences of a school. Some schools also have a list of parents who agree to be contactable.

If you are unsure about which type of school you should be considering, you should probably take a long look at your child, first and foremost. Ask yourselves: What are my child's strengths and weaknesses? Would he or she be better served by a relaxed, friendly, welcoming school or by a school that is more dynamic and competitive? Ask your child what sort of school they think might best suit them. Speak to others - other family members, friends, teachers - about their impressions. If you are truly at a loss, you might engage a psychologist to give your child personality tests, which may tell you something you did not know. In reality, however, most parents have a gut feeling about what type of school will work best for their child - and know it when they see it. That is why the best advice at this stage is to visit as many schools as you reasonably can.

CHAPTER THREE
SCHOOL VISITS

i. Do I need to make a school visit?

The only sure way to establish whether a school is right for your child is to visit it. If you are seriously interested in a school, you will probably want to visit it more than once. You need to see the school in action and talk to the teachers. You need to form an opinion of its cohort of pupils. Most importantly, you need to get a feel for the ethos of the school: the values that will be passed on to your child, not merely by the school itself, but by the children that your child will be spending his or her time with. Many schools in the UK have distinctive characters, which the staff will be pleased to tell you about, should you enquire.

The standard practice for visits to the school by prospective parents is for an initial visit on an open day and then a further, booked school tour when the school is operation, either singly or in groups. Make sure you book early for these tours or you may find that you miss the opportunity. The school can only schedule so many tours during the year - they are very disruptive to the normal operations of the school - and they fill up fast. Some schools conduct tours all year around. Schools with 11+ entry usually conduct the tours in the months leading up to the deadline for registration in November. Many schools, particularly boarding schools, will conduct individual tours at other times, to suit parents.

You will make much better use of a school visit if you have done the basic research beforehand, so that you do not waste time asking questions that could easily have been answered with a trip to the school's website. Establish in advance such basic things as: the size and history of the school, its facilities, its curriculum, its GCSE, A-level and/or IB results, the general outlines of the admissions process and so on. Read the report of the school by the Independent Schools Inspectorate, which will tell you a great deal more. Then use the school visits as a way of drilling down, to find out about the underlying nature of the school and the type of child to whom it is best suited. Make notes in advance of questions to ask.

There may be some advantage in taking a preliminary tour of a school without having your child in attendance. You do not want your child to fall in love with a school that, for one reason or another, you refuse to countenance. Either way, your child should most certainly visit the schools for which they will be seeking entry, if only so that they start to realise what is at stake in their exam preparation.

The function of the school visit is not merely to find out about the school. The school will in turn gauge your interest in it by the effort you have put in to seeing the school in action. There may be a question on the Registration Form asking about your previous contact with the school. And, when it comes to your child's interview, he or she can fully expect a question: 'When you came to visit the school, is there anything you particularly liked about it?' If your child hasn't yet visited the school, there will be nothing to talk about. If they have, then of course the correct answer is 'Yes!' - with evidence to support. Anecdotal evidence suggests that some schools are more inclined to make an offer where they know it will be accepted. How do Registrars know when an offer will be accepted? They can only know it by the enthusiasm shown by applicants. Inversely, a school may be wary of offering a place to a child who has not visited it.

ii. What questions should I ask?

(At the end of this book is a copy of a form that you can use for keeping a record of your school visits. You can also download the form from the Independent Junction website.)

a. The open day visit

Many schools hold open days, which are very well-attended. These are often a parent's first visit to the school. Usually, the Head will speak about the character of the school and give some details of the admissions process. A parent at the school may also speak, and sometimes a prefect or other pupil. A tour of the school will be given, often conducted by a school pupil. Work will be available to peruse; exhibits will be on the walls and in the art rooms; the school choir or orchestra may present a short concert. The school will be trying to show itself at its best.

The disadvantage of these open days is that they are so well-attended that you may feel like a part of a herd. Another disadvantage is that the school is trying to impress, so everyone will be more well-dressed and well-behaved than usual. The school should also be more well-presented, with flowers in vases and brownies cooking in the kitchens. The advantage of these open days is that it gives you an opportunity to address questions to a pupil or a parent of the school. Make use of this opportunity. You may get a straighter answer to a pertinent question from a pupil than from anyone else. If there is a parent speaker, use the opportunity to ask how they find the school and

THE 11+ AND 13+ HANDBOOK

its pupils, and if there is anything that they are less happy with. You can even ask for advice on making an application to the school: what type of child does the school look for? The schools cannot as a rule vet parent speakers, so they will probably tell you something that is close to the truth. Ask pointed questions.

What can be achieved on an open day? The questions below ask for information that can be gleaned simply by *observing* a school: by looking at the classrooms, the facilities and so on. Pay particular attention to the noticeboards: there should be a wealth of information about clubs, sporting activities, concerts, school trips and so on. There should also be some information also what the pupils are achieving outside the school.

Look at the fabric of the school:
　　Is it clean and tidy? Is it light and well-aired?
　　Is it the type of place you can imagine your child spending many,
　　　　many hours?

Look at the facilities:
　　Library - Does the Library appear to be used?
　　　　Are the books being read?
　　　　Do the books support the subjects in the curriculum?
　　　　　　(If the school teaches Spanish to A-levels, for example, how
　　　　　　many Spanish books are on the shelves?)
　　Science Labs - Are the labs tidy?
　　　　Does the equipment look well-maintained?
　　　　Are there interesting teaching materials on the walls?
　　Sports facilities - What sports are on offer? On- or off-site?
　　　　What sports does the school compete in? Against whom?
　　　　How many children appear to be participating in sports?
　　IT facilities - Are facilities freely available for pupils to use?
　　　　Does the school have an intranet and what is available on it?
　　Music, Art and Drama facilities - Are music teachers available on-site?
　　　　Are lessons within school hours or without?
　　　　Are there practice rooms available for children to use?
　　　　How many and what kind of school productions are staged?
　　　　How many children are involved in these drama productions?
　　　　How many choirs are there? Can anyone join?
　　　　Is there a chamber choir for the more talented singers?
　　　　How large is the orchestra? Are there concerts? What kind?
　　Classrooms - Are the classrooms neat and tidy, bright and cheery?
　　　　Is there enough room for the children?
　　Kitchens and cafeteria - Are they clean? What food is being served?

THE 11+ AND 13+ HANDBOOK

In the classrooms, look at the quality of the work on show:
> What is the quality of the material on the walls of the classrooms? Does it look inspiring?
> Does the work displayed show evidence that the pupils are being challenged and inspired?

In the hallways, look at the noticeboards:
> What activities and events are advertised?
> Is there a wide variety of clubs, artistic and sporting events?
> What is the level of participation in these activities?
> Are children's other achievements - outside the school - also being celebrated on the noticeboards?

Study the children at the school:
> Do they appear happy to be at school? Do they smile?
> Do they appear to be proud of their school?
> > Do they wear their uniform with pride?
> Do the children appear self-composed and self-disciplined - or are they rowdy?
> Do the children move around the school with confidence and a sense of purpose?

Study the behaviour of the children towards each other:
> How do the children behave towards each other?
> Are they courteous and friendly?
> Do they appear to enjoy each other's company?

Study the behaviour of the children towards their teachers:
> Do they appear pleased to see their teachers?
> Do they seem to like them?
> Do they speak of them and to them with respect?

Talk to the teachers:
> Do they appear open and approachable?
> Do they appear enthusiastic about the subjects they teach?
> Do they appear enthusiastic about the school and its pupils?

There will be a 'buzz' in a vibrant school, especially on an open day. The children will appear happy, confident, proud of their school and pleased to speak well of it. They will appear enthusiastic about their studies and their extra-curricular activities. (Again, enthusiasm is difficult for a child to simulate, so if they appear to be enthusiastic, they probably are.) Inversely, where a school is failing its children, those children will appear bored, ambivalent about their work, uninterested in their extra-curricular activities and not particularly eager to speak well of their school.

One of the particular advantages of an open day is that you may be taken on a tour by a school pupil. This will give you a chance to quiz them on their experience of the school: what do they like most about it? Is there anything about it that they are less keen on? Sometimes, such tours are taken by pupils in the lower years, who may have gone through the admissions process fairly recently. In that case, you can ask questions about how they and their friends found the process and whether there is anything in particular that they would recommend to an applicant. Sometimes, the tours are taken by pupils in the higher years, with a wealth of experience behind them. In that case, you can ask questions which require greater insight: Do you think that this school is suited to a particular kind of child? Do you think that some children are not happy at this school? Do most children stay on to Sixth Form at this school or do they move to another school? Why? Which universities will you and your friends apply to? Do you and your friends expect to be successful in their university applications?

These are some of the types of question that you may wish to ask a pupil guide at an open day tour:

- How are you enjoying the school?
    What do you particularly enjoy about the school?
- Is there anything you don't enjoy about the school?
    Is there anything you're less happy with?
- Why did you choose to come here?
    Is it how you thought it would be?
- Do you think everyone is happy at this school?
    Does everyone have friends?
- Is there a particular type of person who comes to this school?
    Are there any children who struggle at this school? In what way?
    Have many children left the school since they first arrived? Why?
- Do you like your teachers?
    Do they show an interest in you and how you are progressing?
- If you had a problem at this school, who would you talk to about it?
    Do you think something would be done about it?
- If someone was being bullied or made to feel unhappy at this school, what would be done about it?
- Do you ever speak to the Head? Often? When?
    Does he or she come into your classes?
- What sort of food is served at lunches? Is it good? Is it healthy?

- Are there any special events held during the year? Events for charity? Events just for fun? What event do you enjoy most?
- What clubs do you belong to? Are there a wide range of choices? Who runs these clubs, students or staff members?

b. The school tour

Most schools will also offer visits to the school while the school is in operation. Each school does things differently: some schools dispense with open days and only run these tours, while others prioritise open days. The school tours provide the opportunity to establish what distinguishes the school from others. On these tours, you should have the opportunity to have your questions answered by a staff member or Registrar. In the larger schools, which are inundated with visitors, these tours may once again be conducted by pupils, which is good in that you can use this as a further opportunity to pose the questions above. At some point, however, it is best to speak to the Registrar or Admissions Staff in person; there will be questions that only they can answer. If you are very interested in a school and are registering for it, then it would also be good if, by the time of your exams, the Registrar could put a face to your name.

Below are the sorts of questions that cannot normally or easily be answered merely by visiting a school's website, but need to be answered by a person. They must of course be augmented by questions that are specific to you and your child:

Questions about the school itself:
What are the school's greatest strengths?
What distinguishes the school from others?
What plans for future development are there for the school?
How long has the Head been at the school?
How many pupils continue in this school at Sixth Form?
Do many pupils leave after GCSE? Where do they go?

Questions about the classes and teaching:
What is the maximum size of a class? At Year 7? And at Year 12?
Are the children placed in forms?
Do these forms change every year or remain the same?
Do the children have a form room? Do these change every year?
Are the children placed in houses?
What activities take place in these houses?

THE 11+ AND 13+ HANDBOOK

Do the children have individual tutors, beyond their subject teachers?
  If so, what are the tutor's responsibilities?
Does the school have an intranet and are programs the child needs
  available on it? (Increasingly, pupils will be asked to present their
  work using programs you may not have at home. Can they access
  these programs through the school's intranet?)

Questions about study and assessment:
  How are the children assessed?
    How often are they tested? In what ways?
  How often are parent/teacher meetings held?
  How often are reports sent home?
  Are the children placed in 'sets' or streamed?
    If so, how easy is it to move sets?
  Can a child be in different sets in different subjects?
    (i.e., Set A in a stronger subject and Set C in a weaker subject.)
  What degree of flexibility is there in the subjects a child can take?
  Can a child take any combination of subjects on offer?
  Is the school stronger in some subjects than others?
    How is this shown in the school's marks?
  If I were concerned about my child's academic progress, whom
    would I contact?
  Do you give special support to pupils who are struggling? How?
  Does the school have a program for gifted and talented pupils?
  What grade must a child achieve in GCSE to be allowed to continue
    in that subject at Sixth Form?
  How does the school support Oxbridge applicants at A-level?

Questions about pastoral issues:
  Is there a program for older children to mentor younger children?
  What happens if a child is having a problem in the school (for
    example, if he or she is being bullied)?
  Is there a school counsellor? Is he or she on staff?
  Who does a child or parent approach with a problem?
    What are the procedures for dealing with a problem?
  What are the disciplinary procedures within the school?
  Is the school prepared to expel a disruptive child?

Questions about extra-curricular activities:
  How are pupils encouraged to participate in extra-curricular activities?
  Which extra-curricular activities are pupils expected to take part in?
    When are these activities conducted? Outside school hours?
    Are any sports compulsory? For how long?

Do you have sports clubs for children not in the A or B teams?
How many days in a week do children normally play sport?
How many/what kind of school productions are staged during a year?
Can anyone who wants play in an orchestra?
What grade must you achieve to join the orchestra?
Can anyone who wants sing in the school choir?
Where does the choir sing and how often?
Does the school have a program for the Duke of Edinburgh Awards?
Do you have a program of outside speakers coming to the school?
How often do speakers come? Who has spoken?

Questions about practical and other issues:
Is there provision for a child to come early to school or leave late?
Can a child use the library, IT or sports facilities or grounds outside normal school hours?
Does the school have links to charitable institutions?
What do the children do to support charities?
Does the school have a Parents' Association? What does it do?

c. The boarding house tour

Boarding school tours are often conducted on a one-to-one basis, by the prospective Housemaster or Housemistress. It is important that you have confidence in this staff member, as he or she will be one of the most important people in your child's life. Boarding school tours are more personal in this way and so less direction can be given here. The aim is simply to establish whether your child can envisage living in the house and being happy. In general terms, this is what you might expect to achieve in a boarding house visit:

- Establish how committed the school is to its boarding house(s):
    What percentage of children at the school board?
    Is there a boarding ethos or is it a day school in which some pupils happen to board?
- Look at the fabric of the boarding school:
    Is it clean and tidy? What are the facilities like?
    Are there comfortable places where the children can spend time when they are not otherwise occupied?
- Look at where the children eat:
    Is it clean? Is it convenient? What food is served and when?
- Look at where the children study:
    Can a child use these facilities whenever they like?

THE 11+ AND 13+ HANDBOOK

- Look at the dorms:
    How big are they? Are they homely? Are they tidy?
    How often do children change dorms?
    By Sixth Form, do children still share rooms?
- Look at the children's private space:
    Is it large enough? Does it appear comfortable and cheery?
    Can the children decorate their private space?
    Can they bring their own possessions, such as their duvet?
- Meet the Housemasters/Housemistresses:
    Do they seem approachable?
    Do they appear to be genuinely interested in your child?
    Do they appear concerned with the children's well-being?
- Find out whether the children are busy:
    What they are doing?
    What activities are available in the house after school?
    What activities take them outside the school?
    What are the children encouraged to do on the weekend?
        Is there a program of events?
    Do boarders have any major projects during the year: theatre
        productions, trips and so on?
- Look at how practical the boarding house is:
    How far are the houses from the classrooms?
        How easy is it for the children to get back and forth?
    How safe are the grounds? Do the children walk around alone?
- Find out about the daily routine:
    What time must children wake, do homework, go to bed, etc.?
    When can children change out of their uniform in the afternoon?
- Establish how flexible the arrangements are for free time:
    How and where do the children relax?
    How much television can the children watch?
    Are there some activities the children are expected to engage in,
        such as sports matches?
- Find out about what the responsibilities of the children:
    What duties does a child have within the house?
        At what age do they take on these duties?
- Find out about pastoral care:
    How are children disciplined?
    Who does a child go to if a child has a problem or is unhappy?
    Is there someone a child could talk to, besides the Housemaster
        or Housemistress?
    What happens if a child becomes sick?
    What medical care is available? What are the staff's qualifications?

48

THE 11+ AND 13+ HANDBOOK

- Find out about the interaction of children a co-ed school:
    How much contact is there between the boys' and girls' houses?
- Establish the levels of freedom of the school children:
    At what age can children leave the school grounds?
    What are they allowed to do when they leave the school grounds?
- Establish the rules regarding parent's visits and home visits:
    Can parents visit at any time?
    Can children return home for special events?

iii. Final comments on school visits

Many of the schools in the UK will dazzle you with their architecture, their facilities, their achievements and so on. But, in the end, a school is about the people in it. It is your child's relationships with teachers and peers that will matter most to him or her. A child who respects and is respected by their teachers and peers is far more likely to work to the best of their abilities than one who is hampered by doubts. Your chosen school should treat these relationships as the foundation for your child's intellectual and emotional development. The school visits provide the opportunity to find out about these relationships in the school. Use your time wisely on these visits: do your research beforehand, so that you are not asking questions that can be answered from other sources, but questions that will tell you about your child's prospect of happiness at the school.

You cannot possibly cover all the areas listed above on a single visit, which is why more than one visit is recommended for schools that you are particularly interested in. In the first visit, you should get a feel for the school and have a fair number of general questions answered. For the second visit, you will wish to get a closer look at the day-to-day working of the school and establish whether it will work for your child.

For this visit, it is sensible to formulate a list of questions that are specific to your circumstances. For example: are other children coming from my area to the school? How do they get back and forth from school? Are they encouraged to go on public transport together? Is there a school bus service? Is it reliable? Or: my child already speaks the languages taught at your school; is there any provision for learning a further language, beyond those on the curriculum? Are there foreign language clubs where my child might speak this language? Give some thought, in advance, to issues which are particularly pertinent to you, which you can address in person. Your aim is to have all the information you need, by the end of the visit, to be in a position to decide whether you are interested in registering for that school.

CHAPTER FOUR
SCHOOL REGISTRATIONS

i.   What is oversubscription?

Most children applying to independent schools for intake at 11+ and 13+ tend to apply to more than one school. They then proceed to sit the 11+ or 13+ exams and pretests for more than one school. The result of this system is that many of the schools in the UK are oversubscribed. This is particularly true of two types of school: the most prestigious of the 'public' schools, which are increasingly attracting a strong field of international applicants, and the London day schools. This issue of oversubscription will itself have a bearing on which schools you apply to. Those who are applying to more than one school tend to apply to a *range* of schools - that is, schools of varying degrees of selectivity. They will apply to at least one school where it will be difficult for their child to gain admission, at least one school where it is reasonable to expect their child to gain admission, and at least one school where they fully expect their child to gain admission.

This choice is usually dictated by the level of *academic* selectivity of the school. You should note, however, that the level of academic selectivity does not directly coincide with the level of academic success of the school. Some schools can afford to be highly academically selective merely because they are heavily oversubscribed. A school will be oversubscribed because many parents want their children to go to it. But the reason *why* these parents want their children to go to that school may not be that it is the most academic of schools. It may be that it is highly prestigious, for example. It may be that there are few other schools in the area. It may even be that the school is *not* very academic, but offers a wide spread of activities, both academic and non-academic. Academic selectivity is often used as a proxy for, or as a part of a wider process of, selection by other means. The point here is that schools that are oversubscribed (for whatever reason) will have the option of being academically selective. That is, they will use the results of 11+ and 13+ exams and pretests as a way of determining which children to select for admission.

Some schools do this more than others. For some schools, the exam results will determine their list of offers, wholly or in large measure. For other schools, the interviews and school references will play a greater role. Schools in the latter group may be looking for other qualities in a child, beyond their ability to succeed in an exam at age ten or so. A school may be looking for an all-rounder, a child who will contribute in a variety of ways to the school community. A school may seek children who show an individual talent in some field of achievement. A school may prefer a child who displays an originality of thought that makes him or her stand out from other applicants. Each school will have criteria that match its own distinctive character.

The trick to deciding where to register is to try to find out, for each school that you are interested in, what the selection criteria actually are: is it academic results or are other criteria just as important? If there are other criteria, what exactly are they? Some schools will tell you about their selection criteria; others will tell you very little; and some, you may have the feeling that they are not telling you the whole truth, one way or the other. The schools are of course at liberty to use any criteria they want to select their pupils. It will help you to decide which schools to apply to, however, if you know the criteria these schools are using as their basis for admission. You will then be in a better position to decide both whether the school is for you and whether your child is likely to gain admission to it.

These comments have to do with the *schools'* way of selecting their pupils. It is pertinent here because it has a direct bearing on *your* selection of schools for registration: you must apply to at least one school where you have a reasonable expectation of gaining admission. If you are applying to several schools, it is advisable to apply to several schools with a spread of levels of academic selectivity. It is not worth applying to a great number of schools at the same level of academic selectivity. There is some luck involved in any application: your child may have been in absolutely tip-top form during an exam or interview and so receive an offer which is unexpected. But as a general rule, if you do not gain admission to one highly selective school, you will probably not gain admission into another at the same level of selectivity. This is the first and primary rule dictating your choice of applications: give yourself back-up. If your child is not strong academically, do not waste time, energy and money applying to a number of schools that are highly academically selective.

That said, it is also important not to be put off by the numbers of children applying to a given school. In London, for example, there may be several hundred children applying to schools that may have only 50 or so places available. The situation is not as bleak as it looks, because on average those children will have made applications to three or four schools - and some families may make many more. This opens the field considerably. Do not let yourself be put off by how many applications a given school receives. (Don't even bother to ask.) If your child is truly the type of child the school wants, the school will find room for him or her. There is at present a place for every child who wants one in the UK independent sector. The reality is that the majority of children receive offers from more than one of the schools to which they apply and the vast majority are fully satisfied with their final offer.

ii. What factors determine where to register?

The issue of academic selectivity is of course an important one, but it is only one of the issues that will bear on your choice of school. It is simply something you must keep in the back of your mind while considering the other issues. Academic selectivity will be discussed in further detail after considering the other factors relevant to your choice of school. But first, it is worth considering factors that should *not* figure too highly in those considerations.

a. Factors *not* to consider (too greatly)

- Other children's preferences
  If asked in Year 5 which senior school they want to go to, most children reply that they want to go to the school their friends are going to. While understandable, this line of thinking is best avoided as a basis for school selection. A group of primary or prep school friends can be composed of children with greatly differing personalities, abilities, interests and situations; it is unrealistic to expect all to be accommodated within a single school. It is not uncommon to find that these children have changed their opinion by the end of their primary or prep schooling. Some children come to welcome the chance to redefine themselves in a new school, away from the expectations and assumptions of those who have known them since they were five. All in all, it is best to make a decision about a senior school on your own terms, rather than be influenced by what others around you are doing.

- Other people's opinions
  In the course of visiting schools and discussing them with friends and school-gate acquaintances, you will often hear schools discussed and cast aside as 'no good'. You should try to give as little credence to these opinions as you can. Some of these opinions will be irrelevant to you; at worst, they may be thoroughly misleading. To one child, an otherwise excellent school may 'no good' because it does not offer the opportunity to excel in team sports. To another child, however, it offers the opportunity to excel in an individual sport, such as fencing or shooting. The point is that other's opinions may be motivated by

interests entirely contrary to your own. If you intend to take someone's advice on a school, you should also establish that the criteria he or she is using to judge it coincide with your own. You need to be very precise in such conversations: what is 'too results driven' to your friend may still be insufficiently academic to you, or vice versa.

- The school's Head

The influence of a Head on a school is huge, especially in a small school where his or her values will imbue the school population. That said, it is probably best not to stake too much on the Head of a school that you are interested in. If you first clap eyes on the Head when your child is in Year 5, it is almost nine years until your child may eventually leave the school at the end of Year 13. The chances of that Head remaining until the end of your child's stay are not high, even if he or she appears to be a fixture. Indeed, if the school flourishes as you want it to, its chances of losing its Head increase: he or she may be headhunted by another school. Also, of course, you cannot second-guess when a Head may choose to retire. It is best not to let your opinion of the Head influence your thinking too greatly. A good school will survive through a change of Head. And in any case, what is happening on the ground, as it were - your child's interaction with teachers and other pupils - will have greater importance for your child's day-to-day life at the school.

- The league tables

The Heads of both prep and senior schools (to a person, apparently) will warn you against paying too much attention to the league tables. Why? The primary reason is that the schools on the tables are not judged on an even field: the information included in the calculations of the 'top schools' is variable and can be interpreted in many different ways. This is easily verified: there is a huge divergence in the ranking of some of the UK's top schools on the different tables. Why is this? One major reason is that the qualifications preferred by many of the independent schools - such as the IGCSE and Cambridge pre-U exams - are not tabulated by the Department of Education, so the results of these exams do not appear on tables based on information supplied by the Department. Another reason is that the schools themselves, being independent, can choose to share their information with the Department of Education - and some choose not to. There are other difficulties with these tables, such as the fact that schools may be ranked by criteria which are largely irrelevant to the leading independent senior schools, such as the percentage of children that pass with A-C.

The more fundamental reason to be wary of league tables, however, is that they cannot be used to make a prediction of the future success of your child and still less of his or her prospects of happiness at a school. They detail the results of a cohort - as a whole, on an academic level only, and only in the past. (It will be years before your child's results will figure on such a table.) A school's results may be brought down by a few children who do not perform as well as others. If your child is a high achiever, however, these children's results will have little bearing on the results your child will achieve. (And, of course, a child who underperforms academically may still go on to huge success in other fields.) The results will in fact tell you more about how the school selects its cohort than about what it does with them. This will be dictated in part by the level of academic selectivity in the school's choice of pupil. A school with a broad spread of academic abilities will not figure as highly on a league table, even though it may be every bit as 'good' as schools higher up the table. Contrarily, a school that is so oversubscribed that it selects its applicants on academic ability alone should of course be able to achieve excellent league table results. (And a school that is culling students after GCSE should be even more able again.)

b. Factors to consider in deciding on registrations

The truism often repeated is that there is no good school, but merely a good school for your child. You alone can determine what makes for such a school. Some parents make a list of all the different factors they wish to take into account in deciding on a school. Such a list will likely include many of the factors below. But it will also include further factors that are specific to your own situation. Some of these factors will be practical: location, the extent of the school's language programs; the facilities it offers in support of children with Special Educational Needs; the availability of bursaries, and so on. Others will be less so: your family's links the school; its links with institutions that you belong to or admire; its philosophy of education, and so on. In principle, you could even order these factors according to your own rating system and then judge a school by awarding it points in each category. To some parents, this may seem like rather a good idea; others may think it pointless. Here are some of the factors you may wish to consider in making a decision about which schools to register for:

-   The academic results of the school
    These are important for every school, no matter how academic. The first job of the school is to educate and the way this is judged is by its public exam results. You will surely want a school that, besides

everything else it does, will educate your child to achieve the best results possible in these exams. For many parents, this will be their major concern in their choice of school because it directly affects the next step in their child's life: the ease with which they find a place at a good university. The academic results of the school will naturally fluctuate from year to year, especially in a smaller school. If a school is flourishing, however, you can expect to see an upwards trend in its academic results and so in its ranking on the league tables. Look closely at the school's results and find out in which subjects the school is strongest.

- The destination of school leavers
Where the pupils go after they leave a school is usually a better indication of what the school has done for them than where the school sits on the leagues tables. The difficulty noted earlier is that, if you are not knowledgeable about current university rankings, it is almost impossible to make an informed judgement about what the list of leavers' destinations actually means. You will probably need to ask a senior teacher about them in greater detail. A top independent school will have leavers taking up places in a spread of universities, including a good smattering of Russell Group universities. Such schools will have a reasonable percentage of pupils taking up Oxbridge offers and, increasingly, offers from top US universities.

- Curriculum and qualifications: GCSE, IGCSE, IB
The choice between a standard British education and the International Baccalaureate was discussed earlier. There are other choices of curriculum available to you beyond this. If you have an interest in a particular subject of study, you should check that the school offers it. A smaller school may offer a more limited range of languages, especially world languages, for example. If a school does not offer a subject that you wish your child to study, you can ask whether there is provision for the school to administer exams in this subject, were your child to take classes elsewhere. Another difference between schools is whether they prefer GCSE or IGCSE courses. The latter are preferred by many top independent schools because they are considered a better preparation for A-levels. If you are contemplating transferring your child to a different independent school at 16+, there may be an argument for preferring the same program as the 16+ school offers, whether it be GCSE or IGCSE. This consideration should not be weighted too heavily, however: a child can perform well in 16+ admissions exams, no matter what program of study has been followed.

THE 11+ AND 13+ HANDBOOK

- The qualifications of teaching staff
  The formal qualifications of a school's staff will usually be listed in the prospectus or booklets supplied by the school. At a good independent school, you would expect the teaching staff to have qualifications beyond a basic degree. Many would have a teaching qualification. Increasingly, the younger teachers and the teachers in charge of their Departments will have PhDs in their subject. Having such a qualification is of course no guarantee that the teacher will be an inspiration to pupils, but at least it shows that they know their subject.

- Friendliness and approachability of staff
  Some schools expect the children to be academically self-motivated and approach staff if they have a problem. Others more actively encourage children to interact with staff and discuss their work. At some schools, the children have a tutor, beyond their subject teachers, with whom they regularly meet. The bottom line is this: a child needs teachers whom they respect and have confidence in; equally, a child needs to feel that the teachers respect and have confidence in them. If your child does not have such teachers, he or she will be less likely to succeed.

- The school's environment and facilities
  The quality of the environment of a school will be one of the key elements in your child's enjoyment of a school. Simply said, the school should look good: if it is shabby and unkempt, it will be because no-one cares enough about it. This is especially important for a boarding school; at the end of the school day, a child will want somewhere comfortable and cheery to return to. Some of the UK independent schools are of course very wealthy and boast truly extraordinary grounds and facilities, which will inevitably play a role in a child's pride in their school.

- The size of the school
  Some children are more suited to a small, friendly school, where each child ends up knowing every other child's name. Others will find it stifling and prefer the variety and interest of having a huge cohort around them. Each has advantages: a large school may offer a greater range of activities, whereas a small school may offer greater opportunities for participation in the activities available.

- The school's prestige
  The names of some of some of the UK's top schools have a worldwide reputation, so much so that simply having the name of that

school on your child's CV will help him or her in later life. The rights or wrongs of this are widely discussed in the media, but it would be glib to suggest that this should not play a role in your considerations.

- The priority given to sport in the school
  Sport is played in all independent schools, but different schools tend to prioritise different sports. Some will place great importance on team sports and success in competitions, and have brilliant results to show for it. However, it is best to consider the entire breadth of sports a school offers and whether it has facilities beyond the sports field. Another important question is the level of participation in the various sports: is it the same for boys and girls at a co-ed school? Are there C and D teams, besides A and B teams?

- The priority given to the creative arts in the school
  Art, music and drama should properly play a large role in any child's education. Many children embrace the arts enthusiastically; others need to be encouraged to join in. A school that encourages participation in the creative arts will offer plenty of opportunities for involvement: school plays, form plays, a large choir, concerts on a regular basis, exhibitions and so on. Some schools make these opportunities available and expect its pupils to be self-motivated, taking these opportunities up if it suits them. Other schools have policies which more actively encourage participation.

- The breadth and quality of extra-curricular activities
  The extra-curricular offerings will include a varied range of activities, both classroom-based and outdoors. The range of school trips is something to press for information on: some schools offer many and some, very few. These trips may be the highlight of a child's senior schooling and it is a pity to miss out on them. There should also be healthy range of clubs: everything from acrobatics to zumba, by way of chess, cooking, debating, pottery, philosophy ... But you may need to press for information about the level of participation in these clubs. Many schools advertise a huge list of extra-curricula activities, but few children are actually involved in them.

- The school's location
  Obviously, if a school is very distant from home and your child will attend it as a day pupil, a great deal of time will be spent travelling. This time will be largely unproductive, no matter how much one vows to use it wisely. The availability of public transport will be pertinent, as will transport supplied by the school. Do not underrate the stress

added to a school day by unreliable transport links. Your child should get to school bright and ready to learn, not exhausted by the drama of trying to avoid a caution for lateness.

- The atmosphere, character and ethos of the school
The atmosphere of a school will be a major consideration in your choice, because it will influence the attitudes and values your child adopts during this formative period of his or her life. It will determine your child's chances of success, by influencing his or her attitude to hard work and achievement. As a visitor, the atmosphere of a school can be difficult to judge; it may be simply a vague impression or a gut feeling. Such responses are no less important for being subjective. Be prepared to find that your impressions differ from those of others.

- The school's pupils
The cohort of pupils make a school what it is. Of all the aspects of school life, your child will be influenced most directly by the children he or she interacts with on a day-to-day level. You may form an impression of a school's pupils on an open day, but you may do better to stand at the school gate one afternoon and watch the pupils as they come out of school. What is the demeanour of these children? How do they behave towards each other? How do they speak to each other? Would you be pleased to see your child amongst them? You may find that your impressions of these school children provide greater insight into the school than any prospectus or league table statistics.

- The school's sense of social responsibility
By its nature, independent education belongs to a privileged sector of the population. It is widely held that, for that reason, independent schools have a social responsibility to attempt to accommodate children from less privileged backgrounds within their walls, either by way of scholarships and bursaries, or by way of other educational programs. Most schools have very well-established outreach programs: over 90% of ISC member schools are involved in partnerships with state schools or the wider community and many sponsor local academies. Check what the school is doing on this level, because it will tell you a great deal about the school.

iii. How competitive is the entry process?

Having considered the other factors in your choice of school, let us return again to the vexed issue of academic selectivity. The most difficult aspect of matching your child to heavily oversubscribed schools is that you have no sure way of assessing how academically selective a school actually is. Specifically, you have no way of knowing how well your child must do in the exams in order to receive an offer from that school. We have noted that the level of selectivity of a given school is commonly a function of the competition for that school. In general, then, the more competitive the school, the higher will be the marks expected in 11+ and 13+ exams and pretests. But that is hardly specific. Many parents will want the answer to this question: what sort of marks must my child attain, exactly, in order to be selected or preselected for our chosen school? The short answer to this question is that, in most cases, you simply cannot know. For those of us who are used to doing things with a certain degree of confidence, this feeling of walking around in a haze of unknowing throughout the 11+ and 13+ applications process can be especially unnerving.

For children sitting Common Entrance exams, the school will give guidance of the marks it expects its candidates to achieve. However, for children sitting the 11+ exams and the 13+ pretests, as well as those sitting 13+ exams set by the schools themselves, there is little direction given about what sort of mark a school requires. You are perfectly entitled to ask for guidance, but most schools are reluctant to give out this information. The Registrars tend to sidestep any direct question on this topic with something like: 'We like to gain a picture of the child as a whole.' This is undoubtedly true, but a large part of the picture they will look at is the child's academic ability, as evidenced by their marks in these entrance exams.

The fact of the matter is that most schools give very little guidance at all about the marks expected in the 11+ and 13+ exams and pretests. A school may give out specimen exams, but they will not normally provide comprehensive marking schemes. You will not know how rigorously these papers are marked: whether marks are subtracted in the English paper for poor punctuation and spelling, for example, or whether marks are subtracted in the Reasoning paper for incorrect answers. Even where a school does provide specimen exams, and includes the marking schemes to boot, the Registrar will still be disinclined to give any specific indication about how well your child must do to gain a place at a school, since he or she cannot anticipate the marks that the school's applicants will achieve in any given year.

The point here is that these schools cannot give you the information you want. The exams are competitive. There is no set pass mark, but the level will be set by what other candidates achieve. A school cannot predict from one year to the next what these marks will be. A school may have an unusually good batch of applicants in a given year, pushing up the mark required for admission. A school will of course be hoping for its applicants' marks to be as high as possible, so that it will have a strong academic field in that year. These marks are presumably increasing, year on year, as parents resort to tutors to try to improve their children's chances in the entry exams and as the field of international applicants becomes stronger.

In any case, even were you to know the marks a school expects in its exams, this may still not help you, since the academic results may not be the sole determinant of a successful application. This is the point of the Registrar's comment, mentioned above. The exam marks will undoubtedly play an important role in a school's assessment of your child, but each school has its own criteria for determining which children it selects. A school may be looking for other qualities and skills as well as good marks: a spark of individuality, originality or enthusiasm that will make your child stand out from the other children, perhaps. What these qualities and skills are, the Registrar may not be able to stipulate in the abstract.

Anecdotal evidence suggests that the entry levels at independent schools differ widely. In the 11+ exams in English, Mathematics and Reasoning, the marks achieved by children entering the independent sector range across the entire spectrum, from about 50% through into the 90s, depending on whether the school is highly academically selective or not. Of the schools with an entry at 11+, the most academically selective will be expecting their applicants to attain an average of 90% or above in these exams, with scholarship winners securely within this range. Generally speaking, if you want to be confident of entry into a top independent school at 11+, you should be aiming for your child to achieve 75-80% or above in the practice papers leading up to the exam, in the hope of repeating that performance in the exam (remembering that the child must also do well in the reference, interview and/or activity sessions). You can use this mark as a rough benchmark of what an average school will expect, with some expecting higher and some lower.

Those taking the 13+ pretests will be even more in the dark than the 11+ children, since the schools provide even less guidance on what these exams contain, let alone the marks they expect candidates to achieve. In principle, since children are sitting these tests at age eleven, their marks should resemble the spread achieved by the 11+ candidates. But this is complicated by the fact that the schools that conduct pretesting are generally the more competitive, so the expected marks will already be in the upper half of the range. Also, many schools rely heavily on interviews in the 13+ pretests and the results of these interviews are opaque. You may not be able to anticipate the results of the 13+ pretesting with any measure of confidence. You will have to rely on the advice of the Head of your prep school, whose knowledge will be based on the school's record of success with its applicants in the past.

Those taking the 13+ Common Entrance exams are in a better position than the 11+ exam and 13+ pretest children, in that the senior school stipulates the marks it expects of its preselected candidates in these exams. This is not precise, in that you do not know how rigorously a schools will mark these exam papers, but it provides a rough guide. The highest mark that is required of candidates in the Common Entrance exams by any school is 70% - and this mark is at present required by only a couple of schools. From the most selective to the least, the schools tend to divide roughly into three groups:

- schools that are less selective and expect a mark of 50-55%
- schools that are more selective and expect a mark of 60%
- schools that are highly selective and expect a mark of 65% or more

Because entrance to the schools is competitive, it follows that these three groups will roughly correspond to the three thirds of the ability range of candidates in a given year. If your child's year at prep school contains a sufficiently large and diverse group of children, it should reflect the field of candidates as a whole in its spread of marks. If, further, you can determine your child's abilities relative to this year group, you can also work out which group of schools you should be aiming for: the less selective, the more selective or the very selective. Even if your prep group is not large or is not diverse, you may still be able to work out how well it reflects the norm - that is, the spread of abilities across an entire year group of candidates. Your prep school should be able to provide advice on this, as on the question of where your child sits in this spread.

This range of expected marks at 13+ can also be used as a guide to expected marks in the pretests. In principle, you can work back from these Common Entrance marks to gauge the marks expected in the pretests at each school, relative to others. They too should fall into the three bands described above. Again, if you know your child's abilities relative to the field of candidates as a whole, you can work out (at least in theory) whether the mark your child needs to achieve is higher or lower. So, for example, if the school you are aiming for is the most selective (stipulating 70% as its Common Entrance mark) then the marks it will expect in the pretest will also be the highest - which may be over 90%.

For those taking the non-Common Entrance path, and taking 13+ exams set by the schools themselves, there is little that can be done except to ask the Registrar of the senior school about the marks they expect children to attain or take the direction of the Head of your prep school on this. Many of these schools provide specimen papers of the exams your child will sit, and these schools tend to be more transparent in their selection processes, since they do not want to put off potential applicants. If the school does not provide specimen papers, use the specimen papers of other schools that are comparable in academic level to the school you are applying for. How do you find comparable schools? Your prep school should advise or, in the absence of other information, use the league tables to try to judge the academic level of the school, relative to others. Or ask the Registrar whether the school is comparable to other schools that conduct Common Entrance exams, and then use the stipulated Common Entrance mark of these other schools as your guide.

The extraordinary vagueness governing these selection criteria is something that you will have to come to terms with, when making your final decisions about registrations. The school's level of academic selectivity should figure in the background as you make your choices: it should inform, but not fully determine, your choices. You should consider a school for its other attributes: its atmosphere and character, for example. But the vagueness of the selection processes is a strong reason why (especially at 11+) you should apply to schools with a range of levels of academic selectivity, to give yourself the greatest chance of receiving an offer that you will be pleased to accept.

There is no general guidance that can be given to parents about their chances of success in these exams. The advice that can be given is more practical in nature: prepare your child as best you can and do not worry. Give your child practice in the exams they will sit, so that they know what to expect and have confidence in themselves. There is no need to break the bank on tutors to try to lift your child to a higher academic level than is natural to them. If your child is happy at their primary or prep school, they will be probably be doing well. If your child is interested in their work and willing to be inspired and challenged, they are probably working at or near the best of their abilities. In that case, they will achieve admission to those schools that you identify as suited to them on other grounds. These schools are not looking for children who are extraordinary. They are looking for normal, bright, enthusiastic children, who will make their school a happy and pleasant place to be. They are looking for children who will be prepared to 'give things a go' and give their best while they are about it. If that describes your child, then you should have no cause for concern.

iv. Children with Special Educational Needs

The Independent Schools Council reports that over 66,000 pupils in their member schools are identified as having Special Educational Needs (SEN), of which the most common is dyslexia. It is now increasingly well-recognised that the number of children with Special Educational Needs is far greater than was formerly thought. It is also recognised that having Special Educational Needs does not correlate either with intelligence or lack thereof. Many schools will conduct testing in the first year of their pupils' entry into the school and repeat it at later stages as well, thereby discovering children with SEN who had been previously undiagnosed. If you are applying for an independent school and suspect your child has SEN, you will need a full report from an Educational Psychologist (which will probably cost about £700-800). This will help the school identify the issues behind your child's achievement to date and also explain any lopsidedness in his or her exam performance. The school will normally ask for a copy of the psychologist's report to be appended to your initial registration.

Within the independent school sector are dedicated SEN schools, with a cohort of pupils who share the same difficulties. More commonly, independent schools will aim to support a child with SEN within the mainstream school environment. To that end, schools standardly have programs for dealing with SEN and teachers who are both qualified and experienced in working with such children. Individual educational plans are commonplace, with a dedicated teacher with the responsibility for ensuring that the aims of the plan are met. A plan may include extra academic support, counselling to help the child with behavioural and social issues, and/or speech and language assistance. Prospective parents should inquire about additional costs that may be incurred for such services. The schools will also be aware of what can to be done to ensure that children with SEN are accommodated in the public examinations and will support applications for a child to work on a computer or be allowed extra time in these exams.

If your child has a clinical diagnosis of any special need, there are a number of organisations you can approach for information and advice about schools that match your child's needs: these include The British Dyslexia Association and Dyslexia Action. In the schools, approach the Registrar, Admissions Staff and/or Head in person, to discuss your situation in detail. Having considered the psychologist's report, the staff will be in a better position to advise you about the level of support the school can provide to your child. Beyond this, you will want to establish that the school has an atmosphere and ethos which will allow your child to flourish.

As far as gaining entry into a selective school is concerned, you may need to play to your child's strengths and concentrate your efforts on those subjects or style of test in which your child is most likely to succeed. The independent sector will be an advantage to you here, in that schools conduct their admissions processes according to a variety of different models. Some children may not score well in certain areas in the CAT tests at 11+, for example. These children may be better advised to seek entry to a school which conducts its own tests at 13+, tests which may highlight mathematical or other strengths the child may have. Children who are dyslexic may perform less well in Non-verbal Reasoning tests, in particular, and so may be best advised to prefer schools which do not rely on such tests at entry. However, the individual schools may be inclined to vary their standard admissions procedures, on the basis of a psychologist's report that suggests that a child cannot present themselves at their best by way of these procedures. One advantage of independent schools is that, in the case of a child with SEN, they may stake less on the exam results than on the interview, especially if they see in the child that 'spark' that these schools tend to favour.

v.   Tips on making your selections

Some of the advice below is a synthesis of the discussion of the preceding sections. It is best to set these considerations out clearly, since the process of coming to a decision about senior school applications often involves juggling competing interests. The second and third of these suggestions give an idea of the sorts of considerations that must be weighed against each other:

- If you are applying for several schools, apply for schools at a range of levels of academic selectivity. Try to work out these levels for each of the schools you are interested in, to ensure you apply to schools that span a range that is suitable for your child.

- Do not underestimate your child's potential. Apply to at least one school where you are not confident of success. Your child may surprise you. If you succeed, you are not obliged to take the place offered. Even if you eventually opt for a different school, this acceptance will remain as 'back up', as it were, which may be useful to you if you want to change schools at a later date for any reason.

- Consider your limit of tolerance of failure - and, crucially, that of your child. If your child is unconfident, you may choose to apply only for schools where you are reasonably confident of success. Consider the impact on your child's later schooling if they should feel their school is 'second best' or that they should by rights be somewhere else. You may need to do a calculation here, because it is also a good idea to add a more selective school to your list, just in case you are underestimating your child's ability.

- Also consider the intake of the schools to which you are applying. Whether at 11+ or at 13+, some schools may have an intake of only a couple of dozen. If each of the schools you are interested in has only a small number of available places, you may compromise your chance of gaining a place. You ought in that case to add a school to your list with a large intake. Also consider that, if a school has an intake of 30 but is co-educational, this intake is in effect only 15, as far as you are concerned.

- Give yourself backup, for your own peace of mind. Add a school to your list where you are confident of success. Find a school where your child could go if he or she were not accepted at any of the schools you register for. For example, if your child were not successful at 11+, he or she could go to a prep school and apply for 13+ entry elsewhere. You do not need to make out an application for such a prep school, but merely have it in mind as back-up in case of disaster.

- If you are aiming for one school and treating another as back-up, it is best that the second school is not advertised in this way to your child. In the interview, the interviewer may ask, 'Why do you want to come to this school?' You don't want your child to have to lie. Find a reason to prefer every school that you apply for.

- Manage your own expectations and those of your child. If you are 'aiming high', make sure that you, your child and others are aware of this. Do not make demands of your child that are unrealistic or create expectations that cannot be met.

- Prefer schools where you think your child will be happy, over schools that feature high on the leagues tables. A happy child is much more likely to be successful.

- Gaining admission to a school that is 'too academic' for your child will not do him or her a favour in the long run. Being rejected is demoralising - but nothing compared to the demoralising effect of years spent languishing at the bottom of a school. Keep this larger picture in mind. It is widely held that the best place for a child to be is somewhere in the middle, academically speaking.

- Ask about whether a school has a sibling policy: a policy of prioritising the entry applications of siblings. If it does, you may save yourself a great deal of trouble when it comes to your younger children.

- Do not bother applying for too many schools. Three or four is plenty. Since you will only opt for one in the end anyway, it is a waste of money, time and energy. Applying for too many schools means that you will overburden your child with exams and interviews. Your child may 'burn out' and underperform in the very exam where you most hope for success. The dates of the exams are set well in advance. Check when the exams are and make sure that your child's schedule of exams is not unreasonable.

- On the other hand, if there is an exam of greater importance to you than others, try to ensure that it is not the first exam your child sits. The first exam is usually the most taxing, psychologically. The dates of exams are posted early; it may be reasonable to have your child sit an exam for a school you are not interested in, simply for the practice. Some children sit grammar school exams, in advance of the 11+ exams, in this way. If there is no other alternative, you can stage mock exams for your child. Ask a friend (the less well-known to your child, the better) to stage a mock interview, for the sake of practice.

There is one question remaining about making your selections. This question will bear on your final decisions as well, but it can be dealt with here. Who decides which schools to apply to: you or your child? If you and your child are in disagreement about schools, who has the final say? The answer to this question is simple: you do. Both legally and morally, it is you as parent who has the final say over your child's education. Your child should of course contribute an opinion and you should of course do everything within your power to make sure that your child's opinion and your own are in alignment. Should they differ, however, it is you who decides. Even if you say to your child, 'I'll let you decide,' the decision reached will still be yours and you will be responsible for it. There are psychological justifications that can be given in support of this: if a child believes themselves to be in a position to decide on a certain school, they may also believe themselves to be in a position to change their opinion later on. Such psychological reasons are merely set-dressing, however. Both legally and morally, the responsibility for this decision is ultimately yours.

CHAPTER FIVE
EXAM PREPARATION

i.   Does my child need to prepare for the exams?

For most children, the 11+ and 13+ exams will be the most significant - and the most difficult - exams they will have sat. These exams are generally designed to challenge the children and many children will indeed be challenged. Whatever your child's level of academic ability, there will be aspects of the process that will be difficult. However, there are a number of reasons why a child might underperform in these exams which have little to do with his or her academic ability. Children may underperform for reasons such as these:

-   they are nervous or excited, or are overwhelmed by the emotional pressure being brought to bear on them
-   they are not used to concentrating for the amount of time required to complete the exam
-   they do not realise how quickly they need to work to complete a standard exam at this level
-   they are not sufficiently disciplined in organising their time and spend too long on one question at the expense of others
-   they are unfamiliar with the types of question they are asked in the exam and so misread a question
-   they have poor exam techniques in general: they are confused by, or ignore, important instructions, for example
-   they make other silly mistakes, such as missing questions or skipping pages of the exam

These problems typically arise because children have little experience of the sorts of little things that can go wrong in an exam setting. This is especially true of children who attend a school that does not set rigorous exams as a matter of course. They have not learnt 'exam technique'. Learning exam technique involves finding out for yourself the little things that can go wrong in any exam. These are the sorts of mistakes that you cannot anticipate until you have done them yourself. They include: turning the page before having finished all the questions on that page; turning over two pages by mistake and missing a whole double page of questions; forgetting to look for questions on the very back page of the exam; answering both of a set of alternative questions, and so on. Such simple and obvious mistakes can be devastating, if it means that you miss out on a school to which you might otherwise have expected your child to gain entry. Exam technique

THE 11+ AND 13+ HANDBOOK

also includes such things as remembering to write the answer in the correct place; being careful to transpose an answer correctly from the rough jottings to the answer sheet; remembering to write in the units in a Maths exam and remembering to add full stops in an English exam. Lastly and very importantly, exam technique includes working out the marking scheme for an exam and sticking to it.

There is only one way to avoid the pitfalls of the exam situation just described: prepare your child for these exams. Give them specimen exams - conducted under exam-like conditions - so that they learn how it is done. Some parents send their children into these exams woefully unprepared, expecting natural ability to carry them through (even though these parents would be unlikely to go unprepared into a similar situation themselves). I try to avoid offering a personal opinion in this book, but I make an exception in this case. A huge pressure to succeed surrounds the 11+ and 13+ exams. Your child cannot but help feel that pressure. You may not be exerting pressure on your child yourself, but that does not mean that your child will not feel it: friends, classmates, other family members and teachers will all have made their expectations apparent. More significantly, children are fully capable of exerting this pressure on themselves, without the help of anyone else. Your child's self-esteem will inevitably be damaged if he or she is not successful. To put a child in this situation, and then fail to help with the preparation required for success, is neither loving nor responsible.

ii.   Should I hire a tutor?

The first point to make about preparation is this: it is probably wise not to rely entirely on your child's present school to prepare your child for the 11+ exams and 13+ pretests - no matter how good the school happens to be. Some schools - even 'prep' schools - provide very little preparation at all, apparently taking the view that these exams are fundamentally about native ability. Other schools provide a great deal of preparation, but the specific form of preparation that *your* child needs may be overlooked. (Perhaps there are children in the class with more pressing needs.) Try to establish for yourself exactly what your child is doing by way of preparation and whether it is sufficient. Every child will have aspects of their work that they find more difficult than others. Identify where the gaps lie and help to fill them. (Merely the activity of getting your child to articulate what they have trouble with will be helpful to them.) Your child needs all the help that he or she can get and it is your responsibility as a parent to provide it. Remember that many other children will have the benefit of their parents' input.

The question that looms over any discussion of exam preparation concerns the need for tutors. Exact figures on the use of tutors are by their nature hard to come by, but it is widely reported that in the cut-throat London environment up to 50% of independent school applicants are being tutored in the months prior to 11+ and 13+ exams. The issue is contentious, setting parents against schools and against each other. The general feeling is that some children are being over-tutored, to the point where it becomes detrimental to their well-being. Some Heads have come out recently in a concerted effort to try to stem the practice. They argue that, if your child needs extensive tutoring to gain entry into a school, then you are aiming for the wrong school and your child is unlikely to be successful there - even if he or she is successful in gaining entry. Some Heads express this view at their school's open days: 'If your child needs tutoring to get into this school, then please do not apply.' It now appears to be a question that is increasingly asked in interviews: 'Have you had a tutor teaching you?' It is hard to know whether answering 'yes' will compromise your chances of admission, but answering 'no' will certainly not hurt them. (And lying is not recommended: see the discussion in the next chapter.)

The prep school Heads are becoming more vocal because they see the problems caused by excessive tutoring day-to-day. Some children are being pushed to work longer and harder than is good for them and are being deprived of the down-time on evenings and weekends that they need to return to their school week with energy and enthusiasm. The Heads argue that the price of tutoring is the risk that the child will burn out from too much work, lose enthusiasm for the entire process or, worse, become antagonistic. They claim that tutors' advice often contradicts that of their teachers, resulting in confusion. They claim that children are being pushed to attain higher levels of academic achievement than is natural to them, with the result that they flounder when they get to their senior schools and the tutorials come to an end. These children end up in the bottom of their senior school classes academically, where their loss of self-esteem cripples their chances of future success.

The issue that underpins this debate is that entry for many schools - especially the top London schools - is so competitive that parents cannot afford the possibility that their child may be left behind their tutored classmates. Indeed, you will hear many parents claim that tutoring has been beneficial for their children. The advantage of tutoring is that it is personalised to the particular needs of the child. It often occurs in the home environment, where a child feels comfortable and relaxed and can express their difficulties more clearly and forcefully than at school. The tutor is often a young graduate, with a youthful enthusiasm for his or her subject, and so a perfect role model for a child this crucial stage in their

THE 11+ AND 13+ HANDBOOK

academic development. The right tutor may be able to inspire a child with enthusiasm for a subject where nothing else has. And, of course, tutoring is supplementary: most teaching is a good, so a little more of it is likely to be a good thing too.

There is clear evidence that tutoring may be good for some children, especially those who are underperforming at their present schools or whose schools are themselves underperforming. Children who can most benefit by tutoring are those with Special Educational Needs, for whom targeted tutoring by a specialised tutor is often advised as early as possible. Children who have missed a stage of their education due to illness or some other mishap may be able to make this up more easily with the help of a tutor. The further group often mentioned is the group of bright but lazy boys, who lack the maturity of girls of the same age. Some of these children can benefit by the added rigour a tutor may demand. The last group who may profit by a tutor are children from certain underperforming schools, especially those who will sit exams for the highly selective schools, who would otherwise be unable to compete against children who have been specifically 'prepped' for these exams.

The debate about tutoring does not primarily concern these children. It concerns the children who are already performing well in schools that are themselves good. Is a tutor needed to get these children into a good independent school? The simple answer is 'no': for the vast majority of children, a tutor is neither a prerequisite to success nor any guarantee of it. It is far better to work on practice papers systematically every day than cram for a tutor's visit once or twice a week. The academic levels required at the 11+ or 13+ exams and pretests are not so high that the average parent cannot oversee a program of exam preparation. A parent can soon pick up the skills necessary to mark papers in English, Maths and Reasoning. Indeed, checking answers, going over mistakes and setting targets is something that you and your child can do together. Your child may well enjoy the attention and appreciate that you care enough about their success to devote your time to it. In short, if the aim of tutoring is to give your child a competitive edge against others, then this is something that may best be achieved by helping your child yourself.

If you do wish to hire a tutor, look for a reputable firm. The market for private tutors is essentially unregulated, and there is no way of checking a tutor's past performance, so keep a close eye on your child's progress. If your child's confidence and enthusiasm do not improve, you do not need to keep the tutor on. Keep an eye on the work the tutor is doing with your child and make sure that the tutor sets work to be done outside their tutorial sessions (because a session once or twice a week is actually not enough). Parents should all the while be sensitive to the possibility of overloading the child with work. And they should also be aware that the child's school homework comes first. However, if you are thinking of employing a tutor, first think about what it is you want to employ the tutor to do. Is it something you can do yourself? If you were better informed about how best to prepare your child for these exams, would you do it yourself? If the answer is yes, then become better informed.

Many parents do not adopt this course because they do not know what they should be doing to help their child prepare for exams and so are not confident it will lead to success. If this difficulty can be surmounted, then the advantages of helping your child to prepare are obvious. The first advantage is that you know your child best. You are the one who has watched your child develop and you are the one who has sat through the parent/teacher meetings. You already know where your child's weaknesses lie. The second advantage of doing it yourself is that you set the controls: you can turn the volume and intensity of the work up or down on a day-to-day basis, as needs be. You can make sure that the work is done and that your child remains on track in the program you have worked out together. You can give encouragement and support when it is most needed. But the deeper advantage is this: you are there, by your child's side, showing that you care and that you are prepared to take responsibility for how your child progresses. Whatever else tutors can do, they cannot do this. And this will make the greatest difference to whether your child succeeds.

iii. How can I help prepare my child for the exams?

If you plan to help your child with 11+ and 13+ exam preparation, what you will need above all else are the time and space to do it. You need to be there in the evenings to spend a half hour or an hour most nights and also on the weekend. You need a space where your child can sit down and concentrate on their work without distractions (and if such a space is not available at home, you need to find it somewhere else). You also need the right mental attitude: you need to be able and willing to show patience, perseverance and complete faith in your child and his or her chances of success. You need good organisation, to keep track of what has been achieved and what still has to be done. You need a good supply of work materials, such as past exam papers and other practice papers (see Chapter Ten, below). And lastly, you need the consent (or at the very least, the acquiescence) of your child. Nothing can be achieved without your child being willing to achieve it. Your child needs to be, or be able to become, teachable.

THE 11+ AND 13+ HANDBOOK

How you manage the last of these is up to you. Most children sitting these exams quickly come to realise what they are up against and so will accept any help on offer. If your child doubts the need for preparation, however, the best approach is surely to sit and discuss what they intend to achieve and how they intend to achieve it. You will need to find a compromise. The issue here is that the child must also take some responsibility for the outcome of the admissions process: you cannot make it happen all by yourself. Many parents use bribes - money, presents, holidays or whatever - as an added incentive. These are fine so far as they go. But you may want to ask yourself whether the aim of the exercise should not correspond to its outcome, as far as your child is concerned. In other words, won't the reward be success itself and isn't that enough? A less productive form of bribe should be ruled out categorically: if your child believes that you will love them less if they are not successful in getting into your chosen school, they will be less likely to succeed. The terms of their success must be their own, if they are to be committed to achieving it.

We have noted that the 11+ and 13+ exams and pretests standardly require the ability to perform well in English, Mathematics and Reasoning exams. But, besides knowledge of these subjects, there are two interconnected factors which will determine how well your child does in these exams: first, the length of your child's concentration span, and second, the speed and accuracy with which your child works. These skills are learned and you can help your child with both of them.

At the beginning of your revision program, start by establishing how long and how hard your child can concentrate. Some of the exams set at 11+ and 13+ are well over an hour long. This should not be so difficult for 13+ children, who should by this stage have some experience of sitting exams. Many 11+ children, however, will not be used to concentrating for an hour or more. You can provide a great deal of help here. Find out how long your child's exams will be and start getting your child used to concentrating for this period of time or longer. Start practice early, focusing on the subjects in which your child will be examined. Start with a relatively short period: a twenty-minute practice paper. Then, over the course of several months, gradually increase the time frame, adding more and more work until your child is thoroughly at ease with sitting and working for the required amount of time.

The second factor is speed and accuracy. Here, once again, past exam papers are invaluable. When you first start your exam preparation, you can afford to be relaxed about timing, because the aim at this stage is to increase your child's familiarity with the subject matter and the exam format. As the

72

THE 11+ AND 13+ HANDBOOK

exams approach, however, your child needs to be working against the clock. The exams are typically intended to be difficult to complete in the allotted time, but your child cannot afford to lose marks on incomplete questions. Your child needs to get used to working fast. In English, your child must be able to write both fast and legibly. The only way to learn this is to do it - a lot. Make sure you insist on legible writing in every piece of work set. In Maths and Reasoning, slowly increase the number of questions that your child is required to complete per hour, until he or she is able to complete the specimen exam papers in the time available, with some minutes remaining for checking answers.

All this points to the importance of an exam preparation program, which concentrates on those areas where your child's attainment is weakest. The program you organise will be your own; do not be influenced by what others are doing. Work out your child's strengths and weaknesses and focus on the latter. This program will likely be arduous and it will be helpful to work out ways of making it enjoyable - or at least, less taxing. Break the work into small and achievable chunks and reward your child when each chunk is achieved. Find interesting activities to include in the preparation program, for variety. If done diligently, the process will probably require almost as much of your time as it will of your child's: finding the materials to work on, marking, explaining, confidence-building and so on.

A word of warning: if you look at the specimen exam papers six months or so prior to the date your child is to sit the exams, you will probably be horrified at how much ground must be covered. Do not fret: a child can gain an enormous amount of ground in the space of six months. As your preparation proceeds, you will find that what at first looked utterly unachievable becomes progressively less so. A child may improve their marks dramatically by the simple expedient of understanding what is required of them. (A personal note again: I cannot count the number of times a parent has said something like this to me: 'I was horrified at first. My child was hopeless. But we soldiered on and things started to improve. By the time of the exams, we had it pretty well sorted. I was surprised; I didn't think it would be possible at first.')

How much preparation is needed for the 11+ and 13+ exams and pretests? It depends on two things: it depends firstly on your child, the level they are at and how quickly they learn; and it depends secondly on the academic level of the school for which your child is sitting the exams. It is worth establishing at least six months ahead of time what is required for each of your child's exams and how you plan to achieve it.

If you start some months prior to the exams, up to half an hour of work extra on school nights and an hour on the weekend is not unreasonable. This could be fifteen minutes in each of two subjects per night, for variety. This is on top of the homework the child is getting from his or her school, which must of course take priority. If you start less than six months prior to the exams, your child may need to spend up to an hour per night or more on focussed exam preparation. Whichever way you choose, by the time the exams are looming, your child should be fully capable of sitting a specimen exam of roughly 60 minutes a couple of nights per week and also on weekends. Your child will need this practice to build his or her concentration span, quite apart from the subject-content tested.

Is the preparation better spread out over the space of many months or even years, or is it better done intensively, in a few months leading up to the exam? The answer to this question depends on your child, and on both academic and psychological factors. If your child works slowly and steadily and has a good work ethic, you can afford to start some time ahead. If your child is bright but easily bored, by contrast, it may be best to leave off exam preparation until a few months prior to the exams, for fear that they will lose interest just at that point when they need to intensify their efforts. Whichever way you choose, the focus should be on the last six weeks or so leading up to the exams. Work up to that point in whatever way is best, so that your child is at his or her peak in these last few weeks.

Lastly, if you are helping your child prepare for these exams, tell your child's teacher that this is what you are doing and get his or her advice on how to go about it. Explain that you want to work with the teacher to achieve the best for your child. (But whatever you do, do not let the teacher feel that you are making up for any deficiencies on his or her part.) The teacher may have suggestions about where you might best concentrate your energies. The teacher may have materials and resources to send home with your child that are not easily available to parents, but can be acquired through the school. The teacher should be positive about your contribution: he or she should be pleased for your help and should not put you off by telling you that it is unnecessary. If they do, try to find out what their concerns are and try to address them. Remember that the ultimate responsibility for your child's success lies with you, not with the teacher.

iv. What will the 11+ exams and 13+ pretests look like?

For every exam your child sits for admissions, you will do well to determine as nearly as possible what is involved, and to prepare your child for it, so that he or she will not be set back by nasty surprises. This may not be as

easy as it sounds. Although the increasing tendency is for transparency, some schools are purposefully vague about what their exams involve - and of course they are free to set anything they want, so you can never be entirely sure. Most schools recognise, however, that it is preferable for a child to have some idea of what to expect. Many publish specimen papers for your child to try before sitting for the real thing. Even if the school does not give out its own papers, you can use the papers of other schools as practice. If your child works through enough of these, he or she will gain the good idea of the general range of questions commonly posed.

If you are starting your preparation some months prior to the exams, and before you have made your registrations for schools, you may not yet know which exams your child will be sitting. For both 11+ and 13+ exams and pretests, the best place to start is English and Maths. Standard practice for children seeking admission to UK independent schools is to sit examinations of 50-75 minutes in English and in Maths. You might also start with some practice in Reasoning - especially Verbal Reasoning - since this is also common, both at 11+ and in the pretests for 13+.

a. English

The standard form of the English exam in both 11+ exams and 13+ pretests includes both a comprehension piece (a short passage of text and questions to answer about it) and a piece of 'directed' writing (a short essay written in response to a prompt of some sort). Each of these pieces will be expected to take about 25 - 35 minutes, though these times vary. Sometimes five to ten minutes extra is set aside at the beginning of the exam for reading through the comprehension passage. Occasionally, these two activities - the comprehension and the composition - are set as two separate exams. Also, occasionally, a further set of questions may be included, involving punctuation and grammar exercises. These are usually fairly straightforward in form, with questions such as: 'Circle the words which must be changed in order to make this sentence read correctly' or, 'Add the following words, to make the best sense of the sentences' (a so-called cloze test).

The type of reading text set for the comprehension paper differs widely from school to school. Some schools seem to prefer prose, while others may set poetry or non-fictional pieces such as biography, autobiography or historical narrative. Even where there appears to be a standard format, it is possible that it may change from year to year, so it is best to make sure your child is familiar with each type of text: fiction, non-fiction and poetry. The provenance of the writing will likewise vary: some schools seem to favour contemporary pieces, while others use classic children's literature, such as the writings of Frances Hodgson Burnett, Jules Verne or even Charles Dickens. Again, it is worthwhile introducing your child to a wide range of genre.

The length of the text will differ depending on the type of writing: a poem, a densely-worded piece or a piece of writing that requires interpretation may be as short as 600-800 words, while a narrative is likely to be 1200-1500 words. If your child reads at a normal rate, it will probably take roughly six to eight minutes to read. If the exam format is for ten minutes extra at the beginning of the exam before putting pen to paper, any extra minutes are best used reading through the first few questions and locating where the answers are to be found in the text. Your child will naturally read through the text a second time in the course of locating the answers to the questions, so there is no need to read it through again at this stage. It is important, however, that your child read through every question at least twice, to make absolutely sure that they are clear about what the question is asking them to do. The greatest complaint of markers of English exams is that candidates fail to answer the questions asked.

Remember that every question asked relates to some specific words in the text. If you follow this rule, the task is to identify the words in the text that will provide the answer. The answers to the first questions in the exam are usually explicitly stated in the text. These are the easy marks and your child should take care to gain every one of them. Further along in the exam, the answers to the questions become increasingly implicit, so that the task is to show how the relevant words in the text give their implied meaning. In general terms, then, the format of these answers will be this: point to the words in the text which provide the answer to the question and then elucidate how the words give the answer. The overarching aim here is to give answers that are both clear and concise.

Another trick to remember is that the questions are allotted different marks, according to their length or complexity. The rule of thumb is that, to gain one mark, you need to make one point. However, where a point requires an explanation of an implicit meaning, this will often earn double marks, because it is more difficult. Use the marking scheme as a guide to how much your child needs to write to gain the marks allotted for each question. This marking scheme will determine how you allocate your time in an English comprehension paper. At the beginning of an exam, establish the total marks and then divide these marks by the total time available. So, for example, if you have 60 minutes to gain a total of 100 marks, you have slightly over a minute to gain every two marks. This means you have slightly over two minutes to write a four-mark answer, three minutes to write a six-mark answer, and so on, with a few minutes left over for checking. Questions will vary in value, and may be worth up to ten marks or more, so your child must be careful to allocate his or her time appropriately.

In the piece of free writing that normally follows the comprehension piece, the markers will be looking for the quality, rather than the quantity, of writing. A beautifully written short piece will be preferred to a long, rambling piece. It matters less what the piece of writing is about, than the atmosphere, tone or ideas it conveys. Markers are looking for a good and original idea, presented in language that is varied and interesting. Good grammar and perfect punctuation are essential and a sophisticated vocabulary will earn extra marks. The whole piece should be carefully structured, with dedicated introductory and concluding paragraphs, and structured paragraphs in between. All in all, the piece must convey the sense of having been constructed with care and attention to detail.

b. Mathematics

The standard form of the Mathematics exam in both 11+ exams and 13+ pretests usually consists of about 25-35 questions (some of several parts) to be answered in 45-75 minutes. These range from questions that will not pose a significant challenge to your child through to questions that may be very challenging indeed. The core topics are based on the National Curriculum syllabus for Key Stage 2 Maths at Level 5. However some of the questions, usually those towards the end of the exam, will test this syllabus at a very high level. The exams of the most selective schools venture into what might be described as mathematical or algebraic puzzles, by contrast with standard questions requiring calculations of given values. They assume a mathematical acuity, rather than merely an ability to perform calculations. These later questions may be used by the school to determine which children are potential scholarship candidates. Some of the more selective schools set two separate exams in Maths, the second of which will be much more difficult than the first. (So a school may expect 90% in the first paper, while only 60% in the second, for example.)

As a general rule, the questions in these exams tend to be 'worded' questions: the mathematical problem will be explained in full sentences, by contrast with the more straightforward numerical questions, which require you to work out the answer to a sum. There may be some numerical problems at the beginning of the exam, but the greater proportion of questions in these exams will normally be worded. The child will need to break down the question, paring away the verbal layer to get to the crux of the mathematical problem. The trickier questions do not necessarily require a higher level of maths, but a more acute mathematical mind, to understand what the problem is and what the quickest way of solving it might be. The most difficult questions of all may still require a simple trial and error approach. The trick is to have an intuitive sense of how best to perform the trial and error exercise: where to start in order to reach the answer as quickly as possible.

The biggest problem that candidates face in their Maths exams is that they are often set intentionally long, so that only the most able child can complete them. Preparation for these exams should thus focus on two priorities: practice in the types of questions that tend to be asked and practice in completing the questions in the specified time. Parents helping their child prepare for these exams should thus construct a program for developing, first, the skills needed to answer every question, and, second, the speed needed to finish a paper. For most children, pursuing the first priority will get them to a point of diminishing returns. These children may get to a point where they could, with enough time, answer all the questions correctly. At this point, the priority should switch to the issue of speed. The process is straightforward: over a period of weeks, reduce the time allowed for completing a paper. If you are using the specimen exam papers, start out by allowing an extra twenty minutes (say) beyond the specified time. Then, over a period of weeks, reduce the amount of time allowed, until your child can complete one of these papers with five minutes to spare, for checking answers.

In Maths, as in English, it is particularly important to establish the marking scheme for the exam paper and attempt to keep track of the time allocated for each mark. The difficulty here is that past papers typically do not give an explicit marking scheme. You may nevertheless be able to get a rough idea: there will be a mark given for a correct answer, but also one mark or more for the reasoning. It is important to include your reasoning in the space provided. Even if you do not get the correct answer, you may get marks for the reasoning used. In the Maths exam, the issue of timing is important because is it very easy to get stuck on a question. If a question is taking too long, your child should mark the side of the page and move on, returning to it if they have time when you have finished the paper.

c. Verbal and Non-verbal Reasoning

Many schools conduct entrance exams in Reasoning, because such exams are considered to test native cognitive ability, rather than skills that depend on the quality of one's education to date. They form the core of the CAT

THE 11+ AND 13+ HANDBOOK

tests for this reason. You may hear that your child does not need to be, or cannot be, prepared for such exams. This is not precisely true. While these exercises do not test background knowledge, this does not mean that you cannot prepare for them. The Reasoning questions are very specific in form and there is a great deal that can be done to help your child prepare for them. Familiarity with the types of questions asked in these exams will improve your child's ability to answer them and the speed with which he or she does so. The best preparation is practice - and a good deal of it. The skills your child needs to do well in these exams can be learnt only through practice and that the sort of mistakes that he or she will inevitably make at first are rectified only through practice. Once your child has come to recognise the standard range of question asked in these exams, the task of answering them will appear much more straightforward.

A Reasoning paper for the 11+ or 13+ exams or pretests will commonly consist of about 60-80 questions, to be completed in about 40-50 minutes. The content of the Reasoning exam will be more difficult to anticipate than the English and the Maths, since it is unusual for schools to give out specimen papers. At the very least, you need to establish what type of reasoning will be tested in the exam. The most common type of exam is Verbal Reasoning (VR). This will often include a range of questions that, technically, require numerical and logical reasoning skills, but the issue is that these questions are distinguished from Non-verbal Reasoning (NVR) questions, which have a distinctive diagrammatical format. If you are not familiar with these different types of reasoning, you need to take a good look at them to understand what is involved. Go to a bookshop or online, find books listed specifically for your child's age entitled 'Verbal Reasoning' and 'Non-Verbal Reasoning', and study the different types of question in each. You won't have any trouble finding these books; they are widely available, because they are also used in the grammar school entrance exams. (See Chapter Ten for further advice on resources.)

There is a wide range of types of question asked in the VR exams. One standard formulation distinguishes 21 types of VR question. It is not important that you be able to distinguish the different types. (The '11+' resources that focus heavily on these different types are for the grammar school market, where VR exams often play a definitive role. The VR exams for independent schools tend to be less formulaic than these.) Many of the VR questions are very similar to each other, which leads to the greatest problem you will probably face in VR exam practice: boredom. Unless your child particularly enjoys word games, he or she may become tired of VR exercises long before completing the amount of practice required. The exercises are not so very stimulating in themselves and the questions can

79

easily come to feel repetitive. Try to get your child to stick with it. Each paper will teach your child some small trick to improve their ability to complete a VR exam in the time specified. If your child is getting bored, add some variety to the standard VR practice papers with some spelling or vocabulary tests or other types of verbal puzzle.

The child's ability to concentrate will be a significant factor in his or her success in both VR and NVR exams. Beyond this, the single factor that will most influence your child's success in a VR exam will be the extent of his or her vocabulary. One thing is worth knowing here: for many types of VR question, it is not important to be able to say what a word means, but rather simply to know that a word exists and how to spell it. Therefore, the best forms of practice for these exams are exercises that increase vocabulary. Fast-paced 50-word spelling tests at increasing levels of difficulty are thus an extremely good way to add variety to your preparation program. Concentrate in particular on homophones and on short but unusual words: these recur with great regularity in VR exams. Other word games are also good preparation. Children who enjoy Scrabble, crosswords, word searches and code-breaking games tend to perform well in these exams.

The NVR questions rely even less on a child's knowledge base than the VR, in that they do not even assume a knowledge of English. Yet here again, practice can significantly improve a child's marks in an exam. The questions use abstract figures, requiring the child to work out regularities in a sequence of shapes or patterns, and then chose the shape that best completes the sequence in some way. Your child may be asked to look at a series of shapes and find the odd one out, to add shapes together, or to find the next shape in a series. The variables that may change across a sequence include number, size, shape, direction, rotation, inversion, layering, shading or filling. Identifying which of these variables is at work in a sequence requires you to work systematically though the alternatives, isolating each element of the sequence to rule out the variables in turn. These questions require patience, perseverance and, above all, concentration. With practice, it is not hard to develop a system for working through these questions. Once you have a system in place for ticking off the variables in turn, the NVR questions become relatively straightforward.

By contrast with English and Maths, the marking scheme in these Reasoning exams is simple to ascertain: one mark per correct answer. Again, unlike English and Maths, the answers are simply right or wrong. There are usually no double marks or half marks. Questions do not increase in value as the exam proceeds. This makes the timing easy to work out: the number of questions divided by the time available. The timing in the two types of Reasoning differs slightly: the VR exams allocate up to two questions per minute, whereas the NVR exams tend to allow a little longer per question. But timings vary widely, so your child should take care to calculate the time available per question at the beginning of the exam. In your preparation program, start out by allowing time to become familiar with the different types of Reasoning question. By the exam, however, your child must be working well within the time limit stipulated in the practice papers.

Unlike the English and Maths exams, the Reasoning exams do not in general become significantly more difficult during the course of an exam (though there may be a few tricky logical puzzles at the end in the VR exam). Therefore the task is simply to complete as many questions as possible. This suggests a different approach than for the English and Maths papers. The strategy here may be to move through the paper fairly quickly, answering as many questions as possible and leaving aside questions that appear too difficult. Then, you can return to the beginning of the paper and pick up the questions that were skipped on the first round. Unlike English and Maths, the answers to Reasoning questions will sometimes 'pop out at you' when you return to them.

d. Cognitive Ability Tests (CAT tests)

Increasingly, the schools that conduct pretesting are using computerised IQ tests, called Cognitive Ability Tests (or CAT tests). There is some debate about the merits of the use of these tests in this way, but the schools are under pressure to find a way to select children who will succeed in later years and this form of testing claims to be the most objective assessment available of the factors that shape a child's learning. The tests require no recall of fact, so are held to give children the opportunity to show their underlying ability, rather than the quality of their schooling to date. Being computerised, these tests can be conducted in the child's prep school and the results sent on to prospective senior schools, simplifying the pretesting process, as far as the senior schools are concerned.

The most recent version of these test covers verbal, non-verbal, qualitative and spatial reasoning abilities. The tests are conducted on a computer, are multiple choice and are timed. There are no sample papers or specimen tests. No preparation is held to be necessary for these tests, but practice in the various types of Verbal and Non-verbal Reasoning questions is helpful. Some experience of answering online multiple choice questions against the clock would also be helpful. The tests are now widely used in schools from the earliest years, so your child may already be familiar with them.

The 'Common Pre-tests' conducted by ISEB are a form of CAT test, though the content is represented more conventionally as English, Maths, Verbal and Non-verbal Reasoning. A number of independent senior schools have started to use these ISEB tests as their 13+ pretests. They are normally taken between October and June of Year 6 at the child's prep school. The tests are extensive, lasting two and a half hours, and can be taken in one session or more. The average marks for these tests are set at 100 and standardised for age. The most selective independents will be wanting to see a result of 120 or higher in one or more sections of the test, since such marks correlate highly with A/A* grades at GCSE. There is a very simple demonstration of the test available on the website of the test provider, GL Assessments, available via a link on the ISEB website. Again, both sites stress that the tests require no dedicated preparation. Parents can look at the GL Assessments website - especially the 'Information for Parents' section - for more information about these tests.

v.   Can I help my child prepare for the 13+ exams?

The 13+ exams are of a very different nature to the 11+ exams and 13+ pretests, and the contribution a parent can make to the preparation for these exams is also of a different nature. At first glance, there would appear to be less a parent can do, especially for the Common Entrance exams. Indeed, by the time a child reaches these exams, some of their academic work will be at a higher level than parents are commonly comfortable with: in Maths, the children will have reached a level of algebra which is no longer intuitive, except to the highly gifted; in Geography, they will be discussing subjects that were not even taught when today's parents were at school; and most people have forgotten their Latin, if indeed they ever had it. Further, many children will by this age have learned skills of independent learning that they did not have at age eleven and so will not require the close attention of a parent in their exam preparation. And, of course, the prep school will be doing all it can to ensure that their pupils will reach the required level.

That understood, there is nevertheless a great deal that you can do to support your child towards the Common Entrance exams and school-set 13+ exams. The aim here is in part damage-control: the gaps in your child's learning are more likely to appear when he or she is being tested on a day-to-day basis. The process of going through course material will highlight problems that your child may not know they have and allow them to rectify these problems while they have the time. The deeper advantage has been mentioned before: it shows you care and think that the issue of your child's

THE 11+ AND 13+ HANDBOOK

success is important enough to devote your time to, as well as theirs. For those who are committed, what is more, it is not difficult to 'get up to speed' in the 13+ subjects. You can either proceed at the same speed as your child, looking over the course materials that they bring home with them, or can do a quick crash course before the exams. Either way, if you are testing your child in Latin or French vocabulary, for example, it will not be long before you find that you have learnt the vocab yourself.

It is of course up to you and your child to determine where your help can best be used. The following are some suggestions of the ways a parent can help their child through the 13+ exams:

- Help make a good set of exam preparation notes. Children of this age still have great trouble sorting out what is fundamental and what is simply detail. It can be a great help to go through school notes with your child and get together a set of concise notes of the material that your child needs to know. This is particularly important in History, Religious Studies, Science and Geography, where there is a set corpus of background knowledge that your child will need to answer the exam questions. Go through their notes to make sure that everything important is included. Making a good set of exam notes is the best preparation possible towards the exams in these subjects.

- Once these notes are made, use them to test your child on every point of fact or meaning. Test and test again until your child is absolutely confident about every name, place and date in History and Religious Studies, and every definition in Geography and Science.

- Drill the entire corpus of the set vocabulary in French, Latin or other languages. They must know *the lot*. Help your child make up vocab sheets of these words. Make up lists of words in different categories. For example, in French, ask your child to write every feminine word they can remember. In Latin, ask your child to list from memory the nouns in the second declension, and so on.

- Better than vocab sheets are small learning cards. Do not buy the word cards from the shop; half the learning is already done when a child makes word cards of their own. (It's easy: cut up sheets of plain paper into pieces of about two inches square and get your child to write the word to be defined on the one side and its meaning on the other.) Word cards are a brilliant learning tool: they make it easy to sort what is known from what is not: they allow you to see the progress made, as the learning pile gets smaller, while seeing what still has to be done, by

83

THE 11+ AND 13+ HANDBOOK

the cards left in the pile. Also, the cards are two-sided, so you can test one way and then the other. In Latin, you need only test one-way: from Latin to English. In French, you can start with French to English, which is easier, and then progress to English to French. Your child can use the cards to test themselves - on the way to school, for example - or you can use them to test your child. The cards make it easy to learn 'a little and often', which is the best way to learn vocabulary.

- Word cards are obviously useful in the languages, but other subjects profit by them as well. Much of the material in subjects like Geography and Science can be treated as vocabulary: write the word to be defined on the one side and the definition on the other. In History, a similar activity is to write the date on the one side and the event on the other, first testing one way and then the other.

- Help your child by editing essays. Learning how to write clearly and concisely is something that most children do not achieve until well into senior school. It is difficult and it requires practice. School teachers simply do not have the time to sit down and go through essays in any level of detail, showing where grammar, punctuation and expression could be improved. In English, History and Religious Studies in particular, you can help by showing your child how to write in clearly structured sentences and paragraphs. Remember that the trick is to keep the writing clear, concise and to the point: one point per paragraph.

- In subjects like History and Religious Studies, which require candidates to write several essays, it will help your child to have the outline of a number of different essays in mind, so that they have a good idea what they could write, depending on the questions that crop up in the exam. In theory, an exam can ask anything. In practice, there is a limited range of questions which appear in rotation over the course of several years. If this has not already been done by your child's teacher, go through past exam papers and collate the questions on the topics your child has chosen to write on. Ask your child to 'talk you through' an essay from memory. Assume about six or eight paragraphs; ask your child to tell you what each paragraph will contain, one sentence per paragraph. This is a very good exercise for getting your child to develop a 'mental map' of their material.

- Help your child to 'rote learn' as much of the material for these exams as they can. On the way to school, or while you are walking around the supermarket, ask your child to recite from memory an essay on a given topic. Many of the questions in these exams can be anticipated. In the Latin exam, for example, there is a short essay on one of a limited range of topics. If your child has a good memory, he or she can easily remember three or four short essays in outline. Then in the exam, your child can simply reel out one of these essays before doing anything else, and so have more time for the translation, which cannot be anticipated.

- Obtain the ISEB past papers in each subject and go through them with your child. Look closely for areas where questions can be anticipated and the answers learned. In Maths in particular, look at the range of questions asked on a given topic. Look for ways in which questions are repeated in a different guise. Stage mock exams, either the ISEB past exam papers or from the exam papers set by the schools which do not use the Common Entrance exams.

- If you are preparing for exams set by the schools themselves, look over the earlier suggestions for preparation for the 11+ exams in English and Mathematics. The exams will not be entirely dissimilar to the 11+ exams, but merely at a higher level.

vi. Tips on exam preparation

Some final suggestions on the subject of exam preparation:

- Tailor your preparation to the specific exams your child is to sit. Try to establish as best you can exactly what is involved in each exam. Some schools will not provide guidance about the style and format of the exams, but many schools give out specimen exam papers. Even if a school does not give out these papers, you can rely on the exams of other comparable schools to be broadly similar.

- Once you have established what exams your child will sit, make out a program of exam preparation, so that you can keep track of what you have done and what still has to be achieved.

- Make the exam preparation as varied as possible. Exam preparation in English, for example, may include a range of activities: spelling tests, grammar exercises, short story writing and comprehension exercises involving a range of genre and styles. Even the latter can be varied: one night, a standard comprehension paper; the following night, have

THE 11+ AND 13+ HANDBOOK

your child read a newspaper or a magazine article and answer your questions about it.

- Keep the speed up in each session, to help the time pass more quickly. Clarify what you want to achieve in each session, achieve it and then finish. Part of the exercise is to stretch your child's concentration, so keep the session focused. Do not let it drag on.

- If on some nights your child is tired and not in the mood for exam prep, you can make it easier by doing work that does not involve pen and paper: 'talk through' a comprehension passage or play some spelling games, for example.

- Provide a great deal of reinforcement: at the beginning of each session, test your child on what he or she learnt the day before. At the end of each session, summarise what has been covered and ask your child to tell you something they have learned in that session.

- Present an upbeat face to your child. Try to make exam prep an enjoyable exercise. Do not let any stress you may feel about your child's progress to be passed on to him or her. Your child will not want to do the exam prep if it becomes a time of arguments or unhappiness.

- Note that there is nothing inherently unpleasant in working hard; it is a matter of what you make of it. In fact, there can be a great deal of intrinsic satisfaction for your child in mastering the skills required to do well in these exams. Use the promise of later success as a carrot, but do not underrate the enjoyment of the work itself: the thrill of the 'a-ha' moment when you finally solve a difficult Verbal Reasoning puzzle or the satisfaction of finally getting full marks in a spelling test. Do not subscribe to the myth that academic work is onerous. If you think the work unpleasant, your child will come to think so too and then he or she will be harder to motivate.

- If your child really does find the exam preparation intolerable, think about what is needed to encourage your child to do it. Offer bribes if it helps; do not treat them as bribes, but rather as rewards. We all do work we don't enjoy and we all have techniques for making that work more tolerable. If you are not giving your child the choice about whether to do exam prep, compensate by letting them choose ways to make that situation more palatable.

CHAPTER SIX
SCHOOL INTERVIEWS

Children in the UK who apply for independent school entry will normally be interviewed by a senior staff member or Head as part of the admissions process. Interviews often occur after other exam procedures: if your child succeeds in a CAT test or other exams, for example, the next stage in the process may be the interview. For other schools, the interview will be the first of the testing procedures: if your child succeeds in the interview, he or she will proceed to other pretests or to the exams themselves. These interviews vary considerably, from a fairly short and informal meeting as part of a group of candidates, to an intensive academic grilling by a senior member of staff. Some schools interview all candidates and others, only some. Try to find out in advance who is interviewed and what the interviews involve, for the schools for which you have registered.

How important are these interviews? No general answer can be given to this question. It depends on the selection criteria of the school conducting the interview: some schools value the interview very highly indeed, while others rely more heavily on exam results. You are unlikely to know which type of school is interviewing your child. Furthermore, how important the interview is may depend on where your child's exam results sit on the school's ranking of candidates. For example, if the school has 100 applicants for 50 places, then the following may be true: those ranked (say) 1-33 in exam results will have to mess up their interview badly to miss out on an offer from the school; those ranked 34-66 will have to perform well to receive an offer; and those ranked 67-100 will only receive an offer if their interview performance is exceptional. Since you will not know where your child sits in the school's ranking of exam results, you cannot know how important the interview will be to your child. The upshot is that you will do best to assume that the interview is very important and prepare for it accordingly.

i.   Should I prepare my child for the interview?

The interview process can be a nerve-wracking experience for some children, especially those who are shy, who do not enjoy promoting themselves or who are prone to think deeply before answering a question. Many well-raised children have been taught that it is not polite to brag or indeed to talk about themselves very much at all. Thus the very process of sitting in front of a stranger and talking about themselves at length will be uncomfortable. Anecdotal evidence suggests that this may be a particular

THE 11+ AND 13+ HANDBOOK

problem for girls, who (despite everything) may have already imbibed society's lesson that girls should be wary of asserting themselves.

The schools themselves will warn you against preparing for interviews. They argue that the interviewer wants to get to know a child as they really are, not as the parents would want them to present themselves. They argue that an interviewer can spot a child who has been primed for an interview very quickly. There is every reason to believe them: it must be very off-putting to be presented with a child who appears unable to answer a question for themselves (or worse, is lying through their teeth). Parents should take this warning on board. In these interviews, you want your child to appear natural, composed and fully capable of speaking for themselves.

That said, it seems only reasonable that children will perform better where they have the confidence of knowing what to expect. The worst possible result is surely that your child is so shell-shocked by the situation or flummoxed by the questions that he or she is unable to speak at all. These interviews can include questions which would stump you, let alone a ten year-old. If you have discussed with your child the type of question that the interviewer is likely to ask, he or she will feel more confident and more enthusiastic about being interviewed and so more likely to actually enjoy it. This in turn can only make the interviewer feel more positively about your child.

You must therefore make a decision about what course of action is best for you, taking into account how confident, outgoing and socially adept your child is. Ask yourself: how articulate is my child? How capable is my child at talking responsibly about themselves? Does my child need time to think a question through before answering it? How will my child feel about talking about themselves to a stranger? If your child will feel awkward, think about what you can do to prepare them. Some children are used to having to assert themselves. Children with siblings, for example, usually know how to make themselves heard. Other children may need encouragement.

The proper course of action is probably somewhere in the middle: give your child an idea of the sort of question they will be asked, but do not over-prepare. Take heed of the advice and recognise that over-preparation may work against you rather than for you. A child who appears to have been primed is probably the most likely to be given the types of question that will flummox them. It is probably not advisable to prepare a detailed answer for each question and make your child remember it. On the other hand, you will probably want to get your child in the right frame of mind for such an interview by thinking about their strengths, interests, ambitions and so on.

Together with your child, think though the sorts of things an interviewer might want to know. Get your child to try to remember a few, important things that they might wish to tell the interviewer about: things your child has achieved, things he or she is interested in. Even if the interviewer does not ask, there is always an opportunity to add anything that has been missed. Get your child to think about how to present their strengths in such a way that they do not feel they are bragging, but simply telling the truth. And, certainly, it is best to council your child to tell the truth.

ii. How should I prepare my child for the interview?

Preparing your child for the interview is both easy and enjoyable: all you need to do is talk. While you are going about your day-to-day activities, discuss with your child what he or she would like to say in such an interview. Think of questions and work out answers together. The questions need not be entirely serious to be good practice. These following types of question are not unheard-of in interviews: if you were an animal (a piece of fruit, a house, a machine ...) what type of animal would you be and why? If you were stranded on a desert island, what would you want to have in your suitcase and why? You can make a game of it, while still doing the job: getting your child to think about what makes them special.

If you think that your child will be less likely to open up because he or she is shy with strangers, then it may be a good idea to stage a mock interview with someone your child feels less than entirely comfortable with. An authority figure is ideal. You could ask your present school to organise such an interview with an unfamiliar teacher or you could ask a friend who is not well-known to your child whether he or she would kindly do it for you. Give them a list of questions that range from the most mundane to the most challenging. Add a few quirky questions, to put your child on the spot. Some people even video the interview and then look back over it.

There are other ways you can prepare your child for the interview. The most important is to give your child things to talk about. In the months leading up to the interview, engage your child in the sorts of activities that an interviewer might enjoy hearing about: take them to the zoo, to a theatre production, to the art gallery and/or to the science museum. Discuss these excursions in the manner an interviewer might: what was the most interesting thing you saw? What did you learn? What impressed you? At the art gallery, ask: what painting or sculpture do you like? Why? What do you think the artist is trying to say? Do you think the artist was successful? After a theatre production, ask: what was the most dramatic moment in the play? Which character was the most believable?

In these months, you should also pay close attention to what your child is reading and make sure that he or she is able to speak competently about these books. These questions are among the most common in interviews: what are you reading at the moment? Are you enjoying it? What do you think of the main character? It may be best to choose books that the interviewer is likely to be familiar with, simply to make his or her job easier. Make sure that they are books that your child enjoys, so that he or she can speak of them with some enthusiasm. Also, find some documentaries on various subjects and watch them with your child and discuss them in some detail. Encourage your child to develop an opinion about what is interesting about these programs.

It is not uncommon for questions to centre on current world events. This is something that your prep or primary school may not have covered, but commonly comes up in interviews, so it will help your child to be specifically prepared for it. Sit down and read the newspaper together, so that your child can speak about what is happening in the world with some confidence. Follow some stories over the course of weeks or months, so that your child comes to take an interest in them. Explain the background of these stories and their ramifications, so that your child understands their broader relevance. There is a children's newspaper available at the newsagent, which is intended for children of about ten years old. If you are comfortable glossing over any articles that are not age-appropriate, you can go through a daily newspaper or read the BBC news online. Questions about current affairs are particularly common in 13+ interviews for selection and preselection for the top independent schools. These schools expect children to be reading newspapers by this age.

There are two variations on the standard interview to be aware of. Some schools ask the interviewee to bring something with them to the interview to talk about. This is more common in 11+ interviews than in 13+ interviews, which tend to be more academic in nature. The item you bring should be something that says something about your child. It does not need to be an exercise or project book from your present school, unless of course the school specifically asks for it. If you have some time before the interview to prepare something, a scrapbook of photos, a portfolio of art works or some other artistic item would be ideal, because it would give your child a great deal to talk about. Unusual things may be especially interesting to the interviewer. In truth, it does not matter what the item is. What matters more is that your child has something worthwhile to say about it. Discuss with your child what they would like to take and what they want to say about it. It is probably best to let your child have the final say about what it is, because he or she must be enthusiastic about it.

The other variation you may encounter is an interview in pairs or a group interview. These may be especially nerve-wracking for the shy child. The trick for these sessions is to resist the assumption that your child needs to be the most vocal in order to impress. A child who takes an interest in what is going on around them and then adds a pertinent comment at the right moment may appear more impressive than a child who tries to direct the conversation. Your child should think in terms of what he or she can contribute to the other children in the group. The interviewer may ask: has anyone read a good book or been to a good film they would like to recommend to the group? Make sure your child has something to talk about. The interviewer will commonly give the group a task, such as to try to describe a painting or make sense of what is going on in an obscure photograph. Your child's task in this situation is merely to help the group by adding a few sensible suggestions.

Some schools interview parents as well as children. The interviewer may be the Head or a senior member of staff. They are likely to ask about your aspirations for your child and expectations of your child's school. You will probably be asked how you believe your child will be served by this school. You may also be asked about your home life and how it supports the child. The best advice here is to be clear and articulate on the question of what you believe the school can do for your child and hence why you are so keen that your child should attend the school. Point out the ways in which your child could profit from the school, but also what your child could contribute - without bragging, of course.

One last thing: make sure your child knows how to shake someone's hand confidently and how to say thank you politely at the end on an interview. This may require practice.

iii. Tips for the interview

First, here are some tips to pass on to your child about the interview:

- If the interviewer puts out his or her hand out to shake when you enter the room, do not hesitate and shake it firmly - but do not try to shake hands if the interviewer does not offer his or her hand.

- Sit down squarely in your seat. Sit still and do not wriggle or fumble with your hands during the interview. Smile at your interviewer and look at them in the face when they speak to you and when you speak to them. (Remember to find out the colour of the interviewer's eyes when you sit down and check at regular intervals to make sure that

THE 11+ AND 13+ HANDBOOK

they haven't changed colour. This, oddly, happens rather a lot to interviewers.)

- Remember that, for most questions, there is no right or wrong answer. It is not like an exam. The interviewer is simply trying to find out what type of person you are, what you like to do, what your opinions are and so on.

- Remember that the interviewer is not asking questions to try to catch you out. He or she is simply trying to work out whether the school would suit you. You will do best to 'be yourself'. Do not lie, since then you may indeed be 'caught out'. Even if you aren't, it will make you feel nervous.

- Do not be afraid to let your imagination run free on some of the questions. Take this question, for example: 'If you could be anything in the world, what would you be?' You could answer: a tree, a bird, a dolphin . It doesn't matter too much what you say. The trick is to give an interesting reason for *why* you would like to be that thing.

- If you are asked a yes/no question - Do you have a sibling? Do you watch the television? - it is not enough to answer 'yes' or 'no'. You must tell the interviewer *more* about what they have asked. Do not wait for the interviewer to ask 'Why?' Explain why you have answered in the way you have. This is what you would do in a normal conversation; it is no different in an interview.

- If you offer an opinion, you must also offer some reason for it or some examples to support it. Take this question, for example: 'What do you think of global warming?' You could answer: 'I think it is a great problem.' But then you will need to say *why* you think it is a great problem.

- The interviewer is not only interested in your school work and academic interests. He or she will also want to hear about your hobbies and broader interests, whatever these may be. Remember to mention your membership of Guides, Scouts, or any other such organisations, and what you have achieved in these groups.

- It is not good to appear overly pleased with yourself, but you do need to sell yourself a little. You need not be shy about telling the interviewer what you feel you have achieved or what you are most proud of having achieved. The interviewer genuinely wants to know.

- On the other hand, do not answer with comments that are clearly designed merely to make you look good: for example, 'I'd like to win a scholarship so that I can be an inspiration to my little brother.' An interviewer may find that somewhat hard to credit.

- Do not forget to tell the interviewer if you have a talent in an artistic or sporting field. If you play an instrument, for example, be sure to tell the interviewer that you hope to be able to play that instrument in the school orchestra. So too for the choir, drama or sports clubs if you sing, act or enjoy a particular sport.

- Remember that it is perfectly reasonable to feel nervous about such interviews, so do not be hard on yourself if you trip over your words or say something silly. The interviewer will understand that you are nervous. The interviewer will try their best to do everything possible to put you at ease.

- Most important of all: remember to speak clearly so that your interviewer can hear what you are saying and does not waste time asking you to repeat yourself.

- And remember to say goodbye clearly and thank the interviewer for his or her time when you leave.

iv. What will the interviewer ask?

Below is a list some of the questions commonly asked at 11+ and 13+ interviews. This is about as complete a list as it is reasonable to prepare for. An interviewer may ask all sorts of unlikely questions (If you could be a superhero, what would be your power?) but there is a limit to the amount of preparation that is reasonable. There is a truncated list of these questions, with space for writing answers, available for download on the Independent Junction website, that your child can fill out at their leisure:

Personal questions:
    Where do you live?
    Describe your family. Do you have any brothers or sisters?
        Do you like having a brother/sister?
        Do you fight with your brother/sister?
        Does your brother/sister listen to you?

THE 11+ AND 13+ HANDBOOK

Are you close to your family?
What do you most like to do as a family?
Where have you lived? Did you like living there?
What do you like about living here?
Do you speak any other languages?
Of all the places you've visited, which would you most like to
return to? Why?
How would you describe yourself in three words?
Do you have a best friend? What is he/she like?
How would your best friend describe you in three words?
Would your teacher change any of those words?
Would you describe yourself as an active person?
In ten years, what do you think you will be doing?
What are your ambitions?
What do you want to do when you leave school?
Are you religious? What faith are you?
What does your religion mean to you?
Have you done anything for charity lately? What?
What did you achieve by doing this?
Do you like watching TV? What do you like to watch? Why?

Questions about your hobbies and interests:
What hobbies do you have?
What are your interests?
What would you like to get involved in if you came to this school?
Do you read? Do you like reading? What is your favourite genre?
What book are you reading at the moment? Tell me about it.
Where are you up to in the book?
What books have you read recently?
What is your favourite book?
When you go to a book shop, what section do you go to first?
What do you do at the weekend? What do you do in your free time?
Do you like to play sports? What sports do you like to play?
Are you in a team or club?
Do you like drama? Why?
Have you acted in any plays or performed in any concerts lately?
Have you been to the theatre lately? What did you see?
Do you play a musical instrument? Which one/s?
When did you start learning? What level are you at?
Why did you start learning this instrument?
What do you like about playing this instrument in particular?
Do you sing in a choir? Do you like singing?
What type of music do you like singing?

94

THE 11+ AND 13+ HANDBOOK

Questions about your present school:

Tell me about your school. Where is it? What is it like?

Do you like your school? What do you like most about it?

Is there anything you don't like about your school?

How would you improve it?

What is your greatest achievement at your present school?

What have you done at your school that you are proud of?

Do you have any particular responsibilities at your school?

What do you like to do at school?

What is your favourite subject at school?

What is your least favourite subject?

What have you been doing in class lately that particularly interests you?

Tell me about the last science experiment you did at school.

Tell me about a topic you've learned in history.

What do you use computers for at school?

Have you ever made a Powerpoint presentation? What about?

Tell me about one of the teachers at your school.

Do you have anyone at home who helps you with your work?

Have your parents helped you to prepare for your exams?

Have you had a tutor to help you with your work?

Have you had a tutor to help you prepare for your exams?

Questions about the school you are applying for:

Why are you interested in coming to a school like this?

When you first visited this school, what did you notice about it?

Is there anything about this school that you particularly like?

What do you think you could contribute to this school?

What would you enjoy doing if you came to this school?

What clubs would you like to get involved in?

If you were taught well by our teachers, would you work hard?

Are you applying to other schools?

Why are you applying to these schools?

Which one do you most want to go to? Why?

Is this your first choice of school? Why?

What would be the advantage of going to this school as opposed to another one?

What is the difference between your school and this school?

Do you think they are very different?

Do you think you might have any difficulties at this school?

Do you know anyone at this school?

What type of friends would you most like to make at this school?

Are you nervous about starting senior school?

Is there anything you are particularly nervous about?

THE 11+ AND 13+ HANDBOOK

General questions:

If you could hold a dinner party and invite any two guests (anyone at
all, alive or dead), who would you ask?
If you could go back in time, which period would you go back to?
If you could be anyone for a day, who would you be?
Who is your hero? Why?
Do you have anyone who is an inspiration to you?
If you were given £100, what would you do with it?
If I gave you £1000 for charity, which charity would you give it to?
If you could have one wish, what would it be?
Do you read the news? Which newspaper/website?
Can you tell me what is happening in the world at the moment?
What has caught your eye in the news this week?
Has anything annoyed you in the news recently?

Questions designed to challenge:

What is the most significant event to have taken place in the world
recently, do you think?
Take me on a trip around the world and tell me what has been
happening lately.
What is the greatest problem facing the world at present, do you think?
If you were the Prime Minister of this country, what would you most
want to achieve?
If you could invent a new religion, what would be its main principle?
Describe something you think might be a good invention.
Why would it be good?
Do you think it is important to be nice to people? Why?
What do you think is the purpose of reading?
What do you think about global warming?

Questions asked in a group session:

Do you have an interesting hobby that you can describe to the group?
Have you read a good book that you can recommend to the group?
Questions asked about a photo:
Can you tell me what is going on in this photo?
What do you see in this picture?
Is there anything about this photo that is odd or interesting?
Questions asked about an image of a painting:
What is eye-catching about this painting?
When do you think this was painted? What makes you think so?
Tell me about this painting: the perspective, the composition, etc.
Many people find this painting interesting; can you think why?

Questions about something a child has brought to the interview:
    That looks interesting. Can you tell me about it?
        What does it show about you? Why are you proud of it?
        When you are older, what will you think of it?

Final questions:
    Is there anything about yourself you still want to tell us about?
    Do you have any questions for me?

v.   Is it OK to lie in an interview?

If you go onto a forum where parents discuss the independent school interviews, you will find two questions surfacing time and again. The first is this: is it ever acceptable to encourage a child to lie in an interview? The second is related: should my child admit that he or she is being tutored for the exams? If you read further, you will discover that many parents are coaching their children to 'bend the truth' in these interviews. This instruction is now widely circulated among parents: do not let your child admit in an interview that he or she has received tutoring. Also, never admit it yourself, if you too are interviewed.

The general problem with lying in an interview is that it will undermine your child's confidence. The child can easily become forgetful or confused about what they are meant to be untruthful about and what they are meant to be truthful about. Children are not very good at lying, as a rule, and the interviewer will be practiced at posing questions in such a way as to expose a lie. If the interviewer thinks the child is lying, he or she may continue probing until the lie is exposed. It must be most off-putting for an interviewer to confront a child whom he or she believes to be dishonest. The stakes in this are high: your child is unlikely to get into a highly selective school on the basis of exam results alone; the interview is critical. If the interviewer believes your child is lying about one thing, then he or she may feel disinclined to believe anything else your child has to say.

If you are planning to employ a tutor, you may wish to give this issue some thought. The Heads are becoming increasingly opposed to tutors and children are being asked at interview whether they have received tutoring. It is possible that any improvement in a child's marks that is attributable to a tutor will be cancelled out in the interview, either when the child admits that he or she has been tutored or when he or she lies about it unsuccessfully. It may be better to pursue a policy of strict honesty and give your child nothing to be dishonest about. It may simply be the safest approach.

The other question to which you or your child may wish to respond with a lie is this: is this is your first choice of school? This question is often asked and it is reasonable to assume that interviewers do not generally like to feel that their school is being treated as back-up. The interviewer is human; he or she will feel more inclined to accommodate a child who is truly committed to the school and who wants above all to be part of the school community. What do you reply if the school is not in fact your first choice, but you still wish to be taken seriously for it, even if only as back-up? In this situation, there is no need to lie. Parents confronted with this question may be able to respond truthfully that it is the favourite of one or other of the parents, but not both. They may be able to say that it is a favourite of the parents, but not the child. They can always reply that it is favoured for this or that reason, but not for others.

The best response to such a question, however, may be something like this: 'We have been wary of making choices, for fear that our child may be disappointed. Each of the schools we have registered for is an excellent school and we would be thrilled to receive an offer from any of them.' A child confronted by this question can make a response along these same lines. They can truthfully report that it is all very confusing, because all these schools appear to be excellent, but that they very much like X and Y about this school and so would very much like to be offered a place. This is an excellent opportunity to teach your child tact. It will not go astray in the interview.

vi. Advice for interviews at the top independents

For some schools, the interviews are really only a way of establishing that the child does not have two heads. For the highly selective schools, however, the interview may make or break your application. These schools will be more likely to ask questions that will challenge the child: questions about the child's ambitions, questions about what is going on in the world at the moment, and questions about the relationship between the two - about how the child expects to go about achieving these ambitions in the world as it is at the moment.

For these schools, the trick is this: think of the interview in its larger framework. The schools usually choose the more experienced teachers for these interviews. These teachers will have seen some pupils go all the way through school and come out the other end. They know what these children will face when they come to the next important set of interviews in their lives: the university interviews. They know that your child, like others, may well achieve the A/A* average that is common among independent school leavers. They also know that this won't be enough to get them into the top universities, especially with increased international competition. What the university interviewers want to see is a spark of that extra ability, motivation or ambition that makes the candidate stand out from others.

One way these top independent schools distinguish themselves is by the quality of the university admissions they achieve. The interviewers are thus trying to identify - at the age of ten or twelve - the children who will succeed at this next round of interviews. That will be at the back of the interviewer's mind when he or she sits down with your child: does this child interest me? Does this child have the spark that will grow in time to become something truly notable? Can I imagine putting myself out for this child? Can I imagine my colleagues putting in the extra effort this child needs to get a higher grade than he or she would otherwise achieve?

The school setting is about relationships, first and foremost. The person who interviews your child will want to know that this is a child who deserves, and indeed inspires, the efforts of his or her teachers. Think about what is special about your child. Get your child to think about it and to talk about what they think they have to offer a school. Once they have given it some thought and talked it over with you, they may feel more confident about sharing their thoughts with their interviewer.

CHAPTER SEVEN
THE EXAMS, THE OFFERS AND THE AFTERMATH

i.   How can I improve my child's exam performance?

The exams are of course the crux of what this book is all about, but there is probably less advice that can be given specifically on the exams themselves than on any other aspect of the process leading up to and following the exams. However, the advice that can be given is especially important, since so much hangs on your child's exam performance. The suggestions in this chapter are perhaps the most important in this book.

For the 13+ Common Entrance exams, little advice needs to be given. All the hard work has already been done in the pretests and the months of study that have led up to the exam week. The Common Entrance exams are qualifying, rather than competitive, so some of the stress will be removed. The children sitting these exams will have sat a number of exams by this stage - they have the pretests behind them, plus the internal exams of the prep school and probably one or even two sets of mock exams as well - so they will have the benefit of experience. The extra couple of years since the pretests make for a greater degree of maturity in the way they approach these exams. Your child needs only to show their examiners that they have kept on track and done the work required of them.

More hangs on the 11+ exams, the 13+ pretests, and the 13+ exams set by the schools themselves, because these are competitive exams, which will determine the child's future. The children sitting the 11+ exams and the 13+ pretests will be younger, less experienced, less mature and less confident than the 13+ children. For these children, it will be a great help to discuss with the child in some detail what they expect to encounter in the exam room. Talking through what will happen in a worrying situation is often the best way to make it appear less worrying. A little 'creative visualisation' may not go astray. It depends of course on whether your child is fazed by exams; some children actually enjoy them.

These are some of the things that you may wish to bear in mind in the weeks leading up to the exam period:

- During the exam period, and the weeks leading up to them, do your utmost to be there for your child. Cancel trips, take time off work, do anything that you can simply to be there, should your child need you. Make sure that you have time together doing normal things so that your child has the opportunity to talk through any issues, worries or concerns. Keep an eye on your child for signs that they are flagging.

- Avoid unnecessary distractions in the holiday period preceding your child's major exams. Avoid major trips that will leave your child exhausted just when they need to be focussed. Your child cannot enjoy them anyway, with exams looming ahead of them.

- Try to reduce distractions and ease the number of outside activities that eat into your child's time. Tell friends and relatives that you will see them again when the exams are over. Give your child the space and time to work at their own speed. Give them the chance to focus on what they have to do.

- Praise your child ten times more often than you do normally. Make sure that they know they are loved - and will be loved, no matter what the outcome of the exams happens to be. Remind yourself often that exams are difficult and doubly so for a child.

- Do not exert such pressure on your child to succeed that they buckle under it. Do not let them feel that they are failing. If your child is being given the message that their best is not good enough, they are less likely to succeed. Given two children of equal abilities, the unhappy child will not do as well as the happy one.

- Do things and say things to lift your child's levels of confidence. Building confidence is one of the greatest things you can do to lift your child's marks. (Note that saying, 'I'm sure you will do well' does not build confidence, but rather adds to the pressure: all you are doing is expressing your expectations. By contrast, saying, 'I'm sure you will do well because look at what you just did in that practice paper' will show your child *why* he or she should be confident.)

- A child - especially a ten- or eleven-year-old - is often comforted by such things as having a lucky charm in their pocket. In the months leading up to the exam, find something that will do the job well - but only if you can be sure you won't forget it on the day.

- In the final days leading up to the exams, make sure your child's work schedule repeats material already covered. Introducing new material at this late stage may dent your child's confidence when it is too late to do anything about it.

THE 11+ AND 13+ HANDBOOK

- Make sure your child does all the obvious things that should be done by people - children and adults - preparing for an exam: get fresh air, get exercise, eat well and sleep well. Avoid stress and arguments. Tell all the members of the household that they should try to be understanding if the child appears jumpy.

- On the morning of the exam, do whatever you can to distract your child, so that he or she does not have the opportunity to get exam nerves. Travel to the exam with a friend, play music or engage your child in a conversation about something totally different (... 'What shall we do when the exams are finished?'). If the exam is in the afternoon and you are taking your child out of school early, take them out earlier still and take them somewhere pleasant for lunch.

- There is not much use in last minute cramming, unless your child wants to spend a few moments going over the things he or she wants to keep firmly 'front of mind'. Your child can go over key points, but no more than that: no more testing.

- On the day of the exam, of course make sure that you arrive on time, but do not arrive so early that your child is standing around amongst children who are becoming increasingly nervous. Anxiety is catching. And anyone your child does not know will inevitably look older, cleverer, more self-assured and more popular than your child feels at that moment. The thought: 'How can I possibly do better than that kid over there?' can be terribly confidence-sapping.

ii. Tips for the exam for your child

During the exam, there are things your child can do to make sure that they do not make silly mistakes that will rob them of marks. Discuss these suggestions with your child in advance. Start using them in practice papers or mock exams in the months leading up to the exams:

- When you have been given the paper, but before you have been told to turn it over, muss up the corners of the pages both at top and bottom, so that the pages do not stick together. This way, you are less likely to turn over two pages together by mistake.

- As soon as you are told to turn over the booklet and start the exam, turn to the end of the exam and locate where it is. Every exam will have an 'End of Exam' sign of some sort; note where it is and don't stop until you get to it. (It sounds obvious, but children sometimes miss the last page or pages of an exam, mistakenly thinking they have completed it.)

- Before you start answering the questions, take a quick look over the entire paper, just to get a general idea of how long it is. Then, establish what the marking system is: how much time there is, how many marks there are, and so how much time you can spend earning each mark. Be disciplined with your time during the course of the exam and keep track of where you are in relation to the timing you have worked out. If you spend a little more time on one question, speed up to regain that time.

- Take responsibility for the time yourself. Take a watch, put it on the desk in front of you and keep an eye on it. Make a note of the time the exam finishes. If the exam is composed of sections, make a note of the time by which you should have completed each section. Do not rely on the examiners to tell you when you have ten minutes left; make sure you know it yourself.

- It is easy to miss a question in an exam accidentally. Before you turn the page in an exam, quickly check through to make sure you have answered all the questions on that page and not missed one.

- Do not let yourself be distracted by anything that goes on in the exam room. Pay close attention to what the examiners tell you, but pay no attention at all to anyone else. Do not try to work out where others are up to in their exam. They may be starting at the back of the exam and working towards the front, for all you know.

- If there is something going on around you which you find very distracting - the sun is in your eyes, your desk is wobbly, the child next to you is talking under their breath, or whatever - do something about it. Don't just put up with it. Put up your hand and ask whether you can move. If your pen runs out of ink right in the middle of the exam, put up your hand and ask for another one. And by all means, ask to go to the toilet if you need to.

- Read every question twice, to make sure you are clear about what is being asked. Be particularly careful with instructions. And then answer the question asked - not some other question you would prefer to have been asked. It sounds obvious, but one of the biggest criticisms of

THE 11+ AND 13+ HANDBOOK

children's performance in English exams in particular is that they do not answer the question.

- In questions that are composed of parts, read through all the parts of the question before answering any of them. The reason is that the parts may follow a pattern that leads you through to the final answer. The answer in the first part of the question may be used in the second and so on. There may be clues in the later parts of the question that help you with earlier parts, if you can spot them.

- If you are unsure of the answer to a question, do not spend too much time over it, especially if it is not worth many marks. Mark the side of the page clearly and/or dog-ear the page, so that you can easily find it again. You can return to it if you have time when you have finished the other questions. Often, when you come back to a question, the answer will suddenly become clear.

- If you have only the time to finish one question, but there are two questions left, what do you do? The answer is this: try to do the first half of both. In English, you don't have to write full sentences to get a few marks: just jot down notes that give the outline of an answer. In Maths, you don't actually have to do the calculation: just write down the calculation that you would do, if you had the time. That way, you may get a mark or two for each of the two questions, which is easier than getting full marks for one whole question. The same goes if you have four questions left and only time to answer two.

- If you feel that an exam question is genuinely ambiguous, you have a choice about what to do. The first alternative is to raise your hand and ask the examiner for clarification. However that takes time and may not help much: if the examiner thinks you are asking for help, he or she will not be able to give it to you. The second alternative is to write out, as clearly as you can, the way you have interpreted the question and the answer to that question, as you have interpreted it. A human being will be marking your paper, not a machine. You can engage with this human being by writing: 'This question seems ambiguous to me. If the question is: ..., then the answer is: ...' They want to see evidence of your thinking. If you set out clearly the question you are answering and answer it correctly, you will probably get the marks. You are encouraged to explain your thinking in any of these exams.

- Never finish an exam early. Use every moment available to you. The only reason you might have for putting down your pen is that you are

104

absolutely sure you have 100% - and that is unlikely in these exams. There is always something that can be improved. If you have extra time in a Maths or Reasoning exam, go back over the questions and redo them, to make sure they are correct. In English, edit your writing: make sure that the spelling, punctuation and grammar are perfect.

Lastly, an important note for parents: it is not uncommon to see children in floods of tears at the end of these exams - the 11+ exam in particular. If your child believes that he or she has done something fundamentally wrong in an exam - missed pages, completely misunderstood a section of the exam or in some major way 'messed things up', rather than merely given wrong answers - then by all means tell the Admissions Staff, Registrar, or whoever is in charge of the exam. If your child feels unwell during the exam, the staff should also know. If your child is upset when you come to pick them up, establish immediately what your child thinks the problem is and whether it is something that the examiners should know about. Do not leave the building until you have determined whether anything needs to be done. If you leave off doing something about it until the following day, any intervention on your part will no longer be as effective. If something has affected your child's performance, the examiners will want to know about it. If the examiners judge that your child's performance has been impaired for some reason, they can make a note of it at the top of your child's exam paper and it may be taken into account later. To verify your concerns, however, they will need to talk to the child. That is why any problem must be flagged there and then.

iii. What happens when the final offers are made?

a. Results of the 11+ exams

The results of the 11+ exams come through several weeks after the end of the exams themselves, so it is best to forget all about them as best you can. The action starts up again in February or early March, when the offer letters are sent out. The majority of 11+ children will receive good news - at least one 'fat' envelope - when these letters are received. Most children will have sat entrance exams at more than one school and so many parents will receive more than one offer. For those who are still undecided which offer to accept, the schools sometimes throw open their doors one last time, in the hope of persuading those to whom offers have been made that this is the school for them. At this point, your child is no longer competing for the school; the school is competing for your child.

THE 11+ AND 13+ HANDBOOK

When an offer of a place is made, a deadline is given for acceptance of that offer. Usually parents have ten days or so to make the decision as to which offer to accept. For some parents, then, the situation is straightforward: they will receive an offer they are pleased to accept, accept that offer and inform the other schools that they do not wish to take up the other offers. Upon acceptance of an offer of a place, a deposit it required to secure the place, usually the cost of the fees for a half-term or a term. Once the deposit is handed over to the Admissions Staff, the place at the school is secured - but note that it is not secured until this deposit has been paid. This deposit, like the registration deposit, is non-refundable. This is the final step in the process of 11+ admission for most families.

However, for some families, the process continues. When the first round of offers goes out, some parents have still not decided which offer they intend to accept. These parents may still make further visits to the schools in the week following their offer, in an effort to reach a decision. Worse, many parents will not have received an offer for their chosen school, so will keep at least one offer on the table while they wait for an offer to come through from the school they prefer. If too many children are waiting for a place in their chosen schools, there can be a sort of logjam. The schools attempt to compensate for this by over-offering, but there will still be a great deal of jockeying for places in the period after the offers are sent out and before the deadline for acceptances passes - and sometimes even after.

For those who are told by their chosen school that their name is on a waiting list, the period between the first round of offers and the deadline for acceptances some days later maybe nerve-wracking. Parents are advised to contact the school to ask about the chance of securing a place. In reality, these families must simply wait until others have made their decisions and sent their acceptances or rejections. The Registrars will try to hurry things along by ringing parents and asking them to come to a decision, politely reminding them that someone else is waiting on the offer they are presently holding. If you should find yourself receiving such a phone call, the best policy is to explain your situation as you understand it to the Registrar and be truthful about your intentions.

For those on the waiting list from a prep school, there may be some advantage. The Heads of the prep schools have a greater investment in getting their children into competitive independent schools and so may ring the Head or Registrar of the senior school and make a plea on behalf of their pupil. It is here that the relationships between the Heads in the independent sector comes into play. If your child comes from a state school, you may also wish to ask the Head to ring the senior school to

106

promote your child on your behalf; many will be familiar with this procedure. Whether this happens or not, it is important that you keep in touch with the school to let them know that you remain interested and would accept an offer immediately, were it made. This may carry some weight, when it is a question of filling the last available places quickly. That said, some care is required: you are advised not to badger the Admissions Staff, however keen you may be. They may not feel so kindly towards your child if they feel they are being harassed.

Ideally, by the deadline, all children should have been offered, and accepted, a place at one or other of the schools for which they have applied. However, a school may not be sure of its final numbers until the actual deadline arrives. The result is that a parent may have accepted an offer at one school (and paid a substantial deposit to secure it) only to discover that their child is offered a place at a preferred school after the nominal deadline. The parent is then in the unfortunate position of having to decide whether to pay a second deposit to secure this place, since the earlier deposit is non-refundable. (Children may still drop out, for one reason or another, well after the deadline; it is not unheard of for offers to be made right up to the beginning of Year 7.)

b. Results of the 13+ pretests

The results of the 13+ pretesting may take weeks or even months to process. The schools' offers should be posted well in advance of the Common Entrance exams and, in any case, by the beginning of March of the year of entry, when the prep school must register your child's name with ISEB, along with the name of the school for which your child is to sit the exams. Ideally, by the end of the pretesting, a school will have identified every child who will sit the Common Entrance exams for entry into the school. The aim is that every candidate will pass the Common Entrance exams for admission into the school for which they sit these exams. For the vast majority of children, this is indeed the outcome of this process.

For some families, however, the preselection process may drag on longer than for others. Following the pretesting procedures, a letter is sent by each school for which a child is registered informing parents of one of three alternatives:

- their child has been preselected for a place at the school, conditional upon satisfactory results in the Common Entrance exams,
- their child's name is on a waiting list for a conditional place, or
- the school will no longer pursue their application

THE 11+ AND 13+ HANDBOOK

In the vast majority of cases, the first category leads to admission to the school. The offer is conditional, but the pass mark is set at a level which it is believed the child is capable of attaining with a reasonable degree of commitment. The stipulated pass mark will be between 50-70%: 50% for the less academically selective of schools through to 70% for the most selective, the latter being considered a very high mark in these exams. Note that this mark may itself be understood in various ways: it may be an average mark; it may be an average, weighted in favour of certain subjects; or it may be a mark expected for each subject. If you are unclear about which is required, you should check; you do not want your child's results let down by a single weak subject. In reality, however, the pass mark is opaque, in that each school will mark these exams with its own degree of rigour, so that the pass mark at one school may be effectively higher than another, even though the same mark is stipulated. The point is less about reaching a certain mark than attaining the level required for entry into the school.

The position of those in the third category is usually irreversible. If, however, you are desperately keen that your child should go to a school that has rejected you, you should speak to the Head of your prep school and ask whether he or she is of the opinion that anything can be done. It is not unheard of for a child to move from the third category into the second. For these children, as for others at the bottom of a school's waiting lists, the outcome of the 13+ process may then depend on the child's progress leading up to, and the marks achieved in, the Common Entrance exams.

The situation of those in the second category - the 'reserve' or 'B' list - is more nebulous than the other two. Some schools will tell you the percentage of children from the waiting list who standardly gain a place in the school. It may be as high as 40%. However, the schools usually will not tell you - at least, not initially - where your child sits on the waiting list, so this information will not be of any great use to you and, in any case, the percentages shift from year to year. Some children will move into the first category over the course of the following months, their place being created by those who opt for another school. Some schools offer the chance to return to the school for further pretesting early in Year 8, after which further conditional offers are made. Lists will be substantially finalised early in Year 8, but there may still be movement after then. Indeed, even once lists have been finalised, there is still the possibility that children will drop out, for one reason or another, right up to the beginning of Year 9.

For those on the reserve list, the process of gaining entry into the school may depend in some measure on the exertions of the Head of the child's prep school, who will in the first instance try to establish exactly what the

108

child's chances are of being preselected. If you are in this position, your Head should be in a position to promote your child on your behalf. There is anecdotal evidence that, of those parents with a child on the waiting list, those who show the greatest interest in the school may be the most likely to receive an offer. Certainly, you should not badger a Registrar to express your enthusiasm or to ask for news: the Registrar will not feel inclined towards your child if he or she should feel harassed. You should nevertheless discuss with your Head whether a letter might be sent to the school if your child were to make excellent progress during his or her period on the waiting list, or become a prefect, or whatever. If, for example, your child should start doing particularly well in class tests, this may be treated as evidence that the results of the pretests were artificially low and that the child will perform very well in the Common Entrance exams.

c. Results of the 13+ exams

For children who sit exams set by the schools themselves, the results will usually be posted promptly after these exams take place. The results of these exams will normally be known in advance of March, when the decision must be made whether the child is to sit the Common Entrance exams for another school. By this stage in Year 8, parents will have had a great deal of time to come to a decision about which school they believe to be right for their child and should thus be in a position to respond promptly, should an offer be made. The only difficulty will concern those who remain on a waiting list for their chosen school. The availability of places at the various schools should become fully clear as the March deadline approaches.

For children who sit the Common Entrance exams, in June of Year 8, the period of a week between the end of the exams and the results can be tense. Some prep schools organise a week of activities or even a trip, to tide the children through this period of waiting. If nothing is organised, you may do well to find ways to keep your child busy and preoccupied. For the vast majority of these children, the outcome of the Common Entrance exams will be good news: satisfactory results and the confirmation of the child's place at their chosen school. The school will not necessarily give the marks attained in these exams, but will usually give some indication of the child's performance as against other entrants. Any such grades will be specific to the school that awarded them; each school will mark their Common Entrance papers by their own criteria. In any case, the marks or grades for the Common Entrance exams are not of paramount importance. What is important is the confirmation of a place at the school.

For some very small number of families, however, this will be a difficult time, in that the marks the child receives in the Common Entrance exams are not deemed satisfactory by the preselected school. If this is your situation, you will have to rely on the goodwill and ingenuity of the Head of your prep school, who will be able to guide you on your options. Your Common Entrance papers will be sent back to your prep school, which will send them on to other schools in a position to offer a place to your child: those to which an earlier application had been made or those which will now consider a late application. The Head is in the best position to find such schools, by speaking to their Registrars. If you find yourself in this situation, remember that it is in the interests of your prep school to find a school that is appropriate for your child. In truth, however, this situation is extremely rare and usually only arises where an application was made that the prep school did not fully support. This situation will normally not arise, where the school, the parents and the child are working together to ensure success.

iv. Some final advice on final decisions

There are two final groups of parents who must be mentioned before leaving the discussion of final decisions. The first of these is the group who receive rejection letters, in either 11+ or 13+ admissions processes. Many of these parents will understandably wish to know why their child has not been accepted at their chosen school. Some may know of children - children whom they believe to be less able or accomplished than their own - who have nevertheless received offers. This will lead them to wonder why their child has not. If you find yourself in this situation, there is little that can be done to mollify your feelings. You should be aware that even the most selective of schools is not necessarily looking for the most able or accomplished of children. It is looking for children who are expected to thrive in that school's environment. A school will have its own selection criteria, which may be more or less well-documented. But it is under no obligation to justify its decisions and will not normally do so.

The truth of the matter is that the children who are competing in the 11+ and 13+ exams and pre-tests do not always compete on a level playing field. There may be factors that sway a decision in favour of some children against others. A school may, in particular, give preference to children coming from certain 'feeder schools' or from its own junior school, if it has one. It is well to be aware from the outset that these preferences do operate in the independent school sphere. The issue is not one of equity: the schools make no claim to treat all applicants impartially.

There is no process for appealing against a school's decision. You, or the Head of your child's present school, may be able to find out what aspect of your child's performance let your application down, but it may not be in your best interests - or those of your child - to press the issue. The best advice that can be given to these parents is to simply move on and find reasons to prefer an alternative school. If your child narrowly missed out on an offer, you may be able to put your name on a waiting list for places that become available should other children leave at a later stage. You may do better, however, to commit yourself to a school which is more enthusiastic about your child.

The second group of parents are those in the opposite situation, as it were: those who are spoiled for choice. What advice can be given to those who are still unsure, in the days leading up to the deadline for acceptances, which school to choose? This advice is given by the Heads and the Registrars themselves: you can look at the league tables, university outcomes, prestige, facilities, teachers and so on. However, the best indication of whether your child will be happy at a school is whether you can imagine him or her as a pupil there. It is a decision that is best made not merely with the head but also with the heart. You will have intuitive responses to these schools, one way or the other, for reasons that may be difficult to pin down. Such intuitions are often the best guide you will have, in determining whether your child will succeed there.

When you come to making your final decisions, remember that your child's desires are crucially important. Discuss your views with your child. Come to your decisions together, as far as you can. The ultimate responsibility for this decision is yours. However, if your child feels that their wishes are respected, they will be more likely to take responsibility for their part in the process. Inversely, if your child feels that their wishes have not been respected, the effects of this will follow them into their senior school. A child may feel less inclined to achieve at one school if they believe they belong somewhere else.

It is very easy to get caught up in the 11+ or 13+ admissions process and start to think of it is an end in itself. It is not: your aim in the selection process is to gain entry to a school where your child will thrive in years to come. The 11+ and 13+ are merely a part of a larger process, of which the aim is success in later years. It is a good idea to keep this broader perspective in mind as you make the final decision as to which school is right for your child.

CHAPTER EIGHT
STATE SCHOOL AND
INTERNATIONAL APPLICATIONS

i.   State school applicants

Every year in the UK, many thousands of children transfer from the state primary schools to the independent sector. In Year 6, these children have the choice of sitting 11+ exams for admission to their senior schools, or transferring to a prep school and sitting 13+ exams for admission to their senior schools at that later stage. For those taking the latter option, there will also be tests for entry into the prep school, which are usually similar to, though less formalised than, other 11+ exams. Some few children move from the state to the independent sector at 13+, by way of exams set by the schools rather than the Common Entrance exams, but this is unusual. Generally speaking, after Year 6, the next major point of transition between state and independent sectors is Year 12 - that is, Sixth Form. Thus the information in this chapter primarily concerns the choices available to parents when their child is in, or approaching, Year 6.

If your child attends a state primary school and you wish to transfer to an independent school with a 13+ entry, you will need to decide when it is best to move into the independent sector, considering the options available to you. The majority of schools with 13+ entry use the Common Entrance exams as the basis of their admissions procedures. In order to pass these exams, your child must be at a school which will prepare him or her for them: a 'prep school'. The Common Entrance program starts in Year 7. Hence the children who will go on to sit these exams typically make the move into the independent sector at the beginning of Year 7, having completed their primary education in Year 6. The same is generally true of children who do not sit Common Entrance exams, but other 13+ exams set by schools themselves.

Some prep school Heads argue, however, that the move is best made earlier, in Year 6 at the latest, to give the child a better chance to prepare themselves for the intensive demands of the Common Entrance program. A small number of schools thus have a 10+ entry (or less commonly, an 11+ deferred entry: a set of exams, similar in form to the 11+, which a child sits at 10+ to secure a place in Year 7). These are more often the boys' schools with attached junior schools or the co-educational schools. The children who move at 10+ may find the transition from state primary school to independent senior school to be smoother.

112

a. Is it more difficult to apply from a state school?

For many children, the difficulty of gaining admission to a selective independent school is increased by the fact that they do not have others around them with any experience of it. The Heads and senior staff of some primary schools have little experience of sending children into the independent sector or may do it so seldom that their information is out of date. They may be able to offer general advice, but not the precise information needed for making an informed selection between schools. If you are coming from such a school, you may need to put more effort into the 11+ process than others already in the independent sector. You may need to do more careful research and rely more heavily on your own judgement than others who have the advantage of a prep school Head to advise them.

If you are sitting the 11+ exams from a state primary school, the most important piece of information you can be given is this: a state primary school in the UK is not designed to educate a child to the level required to excel in the exams set by independent schools for entry at 11+. The state sector aims to achieve a good Level 4 or above for every child in the Year 6 National Curriculum (or SATs) Tests. The independent schools commonly state that the exams are set 'for those at, or working towards, Level 5' - that is, at a level higher than Level 4. But many of the questions in standard 11+ exams - up to half of them - will be set at the very highest reaches of Level 5 (and may even dip into Level 6).

You do not need to be familiar with this grading system. The point is merely that the level of achievement expected by many of the independent schools of children at age eleven is higher - and sometimes far higher - than is standardly expected in state primaries. Even if your child is clever, he or she may still need to work to get to this higher level. For this reason, some parents decide to make the transition from the state to the independent sector earlier, in Year 5 or 6, so that they have the advantage of applying to a senior school from within the independent sector. That's the bad news.

The good news is that, although it may be more difficult to enter an independent school from a state school, in the vast majority of cases, this difficulty is not great. There is much greater movement between the state and independent sectors than there was ten or twenty years ago. An application from a state school will be nothing new to any Registrar of an independent senior school in the UK. The other good news is that, while you do have to put effort into the admissions process, you do not have to go to the expense of hiring advisors and tutors. You do not need an advisor to find out which schools may be right for your child or how to apply for them. All this information, you can obtain by visiting the websites of the schools and the ISI reports, by visiting schools and talking to Admissions Staff or, if you are really stumped, by visiting an online forum and asking for advice there. Nor will you necessarily need a tutor to prepare your child for the independent school exams. Provided you have a reasonable level of English and some basic skills in Maths, you can work out what needs to be done yourself, obtain the materials and work through them with your child at home. You do not even need to buy these preparation materials. There are a great number of specimen exams and practice papers available online (see Chapter Ten below).

Some parents of state-educated children figure that the money that they have saved on school fees can profitably be used at this point by hiring a tutor to educate their child to the level required for success at 11+. By all means, employ a tutor if you have the means to do so. However, it is expensive and involves work that, in many cases, can be done by a committed parent. Even if you employ a tutor two or three times a week, your own involvement will still be more important than any contribution a tutor can make. The independent schools will tend to select children with a home life that is 'conducive to success'. The involvement of parents in the 11+ process is merely an instance of this. Children may be asked at interview whether there is someone at home who helps them with their homework, exam preparation and so on. You want your child to be able to say, 'yes!' with some enthusiasm.

b. What difficulties might I face?

The greatest difficulty that you may face if you are moving from the state to the independent sector is a lack of guidance about the process in general. Such guidance is usually readily available to the parents of children in the prep schools. For example, prep school Heads usually advise parents about the schools most suited to their children and the academic levels expected at these schools. The parents of state-educated children often have very little guidance of this nature and must try to work these things out by themselves. They may also have very little guidance about what to expect in the 11+ exams and how best to prepare for them. If this is your situation, try to find other sources that will provide the information you need. The advice of the Admissions Staff of the senior schools to which you are applying will be particularly valuable. Online forums are also an excellent way of obtaining any information you lack. You will be surprised at how many people are pleased to share the information they have.

THE 11+ AND 13+ HANDBOOK

This lack of guidance may become particularly apparent when you are trying to determine the levels of attainment expected of candidates to the various schools. If you are coming from the state sector, you may need to quiz the Registrars and Admissions Staff quite closely to obtain information on this. Explain that you are finding it difficult to assess whether it is worthwhile for your child to register for their school, because you do not know what academic level the school requires. Find out the level your child has achieved in their SATs testing and also try to establish, as best you can, the marks your child is attaining in specimen exams. Then ask for advice from the Registrar as to whether your child appears to fit the academic profile of candidates for their school. (The discussion of 'assessing academic levels' in Chapter Two is pertinent here.)

There is another difference between children coming from state primaries and those coming from prep schools which you should be aware of: the former often have little experience of exams. Prep schools tend to 'prep' their pupils with exams taken in a more rigorous fashion. The only way to compensate for a lack of exam experience is to set your child specimen exam papers in exam-like conditions, strictly observed. (See Chapter Ten below on how to obtain these exam papers.) Prep school children will normally sit these papers as mock exams, set by their school. Your child will benefit by sitting them as well - if not at school, then at home.

There is one particular difficulty facing parents from the state sector that deserves attention because it is particularly intractable: state school teachers and Heads sometimes have an antipathy (however slight) towards the independent school sector in general. This would be neither here nor there in most circumstances, but the danger is that this attitude may emerge in their treatment of your applications to these schools. At the very least, they may be peeved about the extra work involved in writing references for your child - work that is not required for children remaining within the state sector. (If you are applying to four schools, for example, the teacher will receive four very detailed sets of forms, with space for further, individualised comments. These may take quite some time to complete.) It is not unknown for some primary teachers and even Heads to simply 'forget' to fill them out.

Unfortunately, any such antipathy will only be exacerbated by the questions that may appear on these forms. Some independent schools ask: 'What is the academic level of this child, compared to others in his/her class?' or 'Academically, in what band does this child sit in their class: top, top three, top half, bottom half?' State sector teachers do not generally expect to have to answer questions of this nature. Questions about a child's rank will be

115

THE 11+ AND 13+ HANDBOOK

off-putting to teachers whose overriding objective is to get *every* child to a reasonable level. They may respond that your child is in the top half (when in fact your child is at the top) in abreaction to the question itself. Worse still will be questions about whether your child's home life is 'conducive to success' at school. Many a primary school teacher will be reluctant to answer questions such as these, on the grounds that they patently discriminate against children whose home life is non-conducive.

Because the school references are confidential, you cannot know whether this may be a problem for you. In the first instance, therefore, try to ensure that your present school will support your application to an independent school and that both Head and form teacher are prepared to write positive references for your child. Make an appointment to speak to your child's teacher and another to speak to the Head. Explain why you are applying to these schools. Ask them whether they have experience filling out these forms. Warn them that they may need to answer questions such as those mentioned above and find out whether they are comfortable answering them. The reference is confidential, but you can still discuss what is likely to be said about your child. If your home life is indeed conducive to success at school, highlight that fact and say (tactfully) that you'd be sincerely grateful if they would be willing to report this in the reference. If you are applying to a school where entry is highly competitive, you should inform both teacher and Head is that your child may not succeed in gaining entry without their support. (They may not be fully aware of this.)

At the very least, you ought to warn both teacher and Head that these forms are coming, that they may take time to complete and that you will be very grateful for their help. Remember that the success of a prep school is judged partly on the senior schools its pupils gain admission to. Prep school Heads have an interest in write glowing references: if they succeed in getting their pupils into the best schools, it will reflect well on them. There is no such advantage to state school staff in putting in the work required to get your child into an independent senior school. They will only do it because they want to. If you are thinking about these issues well in advance, you may like to give thought to the question of what you can do for your primary school, by way of reciprocity: helping children with reading, helping with school clubs and so on. Of course the Head will feel more inclined to help a family that has made a contribution to the school community.

If your school does appear less than fully supportive for some reason, you may wish to warn the Registrar or Admissions Staff that the reference they receive for your child may not be as effusive as it might be. You will have to rely on your judgement here: you don't want to create an issue out of nothing. You will not see the reference that your school sends; you may be worrying unnecessarily. But if you feel you have reason to be concerned, it may be a good idea to discuss the issue with the Registrar. The Registrar will be aware that state school teachers and Heads have no particular interest in these forms (and that arguably it is not even within the terms of their employment to fill them out).

Likewise, if you have reason to doubt that a reference will be sent from your primary to the independent senior school, you can always check with the Registrar at the appropriate time whether it has arrived. The Registrar is unlikely to try to track down a missing reference, so you will need to do it. If you cannot make these forms materialise, don't panic: the Registrar will likely have seen this before. He or she should realise that you cannot move mountains.

In this case, you can offer as a substitute recent reports that you have received from the primary school. Although not intended for this purpose, they may provide some of the information that the senior school wants. The school will simply have to rely more heavily on the other information that they have available to them: the exam results and interviews. A last word on the issue of references: it appears that some schools have recently started to charge for the work that is involved in filling out these forms: the going rate appears to be £50. This practice may become more common in the future.

c. Tips for state school applicants

- Try to ensure that the schools you register for have a good attitude to children coming from the state sector. When you take a school tour (especially if it is given by a school pupil) ask: 'How many of the children at this school went to a state primary?' The answer you want to hear is not 'a few' or even 'a lot'; it is 'I don't know.' Once a child has joined the school community, it should no longer be an issue what type of school they came from. The Admissions Staff will nevertheless be able to tell you how many children come from state schools.

- Do not be afraid to apply for a scholarship. It will not spoil your chances of winning a place at the school if you do not succeed. Similarly, do not be afraid to apply for a bursary, if you think you meet the criteria. The schools are actively looking for good candidates for their bursaries and actively encourage parents to apply for them. It is surprising that more parents do not avail themselves of this offer.

THE 11+ AND 13+ HANDBOOK

- If there are no others from your school moving to the independent sector, you will have to rely heavily on your own resources throughout the admissions process. Be particularly careful with your research, because any misunderstandings will not be picked up in discussions at the school gate. Relying so heavily on your own initiative can be demoralising at times, so you may find you need to put special effort into keeping your own confidence up, as well as that of your child.

- Join forums to get an idea of the concerns of other parents applying for independent schools. There is a great deal that you can learn about the schools and their application procedures from these forums. Also, it makes the process less lonely.

- Note what was said earlier (in Chapter Four) about applying to schools with a spread of academic levels, but do not overcompensate for your lack of guidance on these levels by adding *more* schools to your list of applications. Different children have different tolerance levels, but it is not reasonable for a child to be sitting more than half a dozen exams.

- On the other hand, if you have the luxury of choice, it would be better if the exam for your first choice of school were not the first exam your child sits. This point (also discussed in Chapter Four) is particularly pertinent to those coming from state schools with little experience of exams. The dates of exams are given well in advance. If possible, organise for your child to sit another exam first - even if it is an exam for a school you were not otherwise planning to register for. The exams for selective state secondary schools - if there is one in your area - are usually held some months before the exams for the independent schools. You may like to put your name down to sit the entry exams for one of these.

- Do not be put off applying to an independent school on the basis that your child will be unlike the other children in the school because you are not as wealthy (or as ... anything else) as other families. Most independent schools have a great variety of children, of diverse backgrounds, nationalities, levels of privilege and so on. If your child is successful at his or her school, your wealth (or lack of it) will not be an issue.

- Do not be put off applying to an independent school by any antipathy towards the independent sector others may express. Others are welcome to hold their opinions; nothing compels you to share them.

118

- Finally, although your child may be disadvantaged in some ways in these exams, as against children already in the independent sector, do not feel tempted to make too much of this. Some prep schools provide very little 'preparation' at all. And some children at these schools are so privileged that they have yet to learn that some things require hard work. Those children are arguably more disadvantaged than yours.

ii. International applicants

Increasingly, students are coming to the UK from overseas to be educated in some of the best schools in the world. The Independent Schools Council reports that there are presently 26,000 international students studying in its member schools (which represent 80% of UK independent schools) and numbers are increasing annually. In some of the UK's boarding schools, the number of international students has risen to above 25% of the school cohort. Indeed, the independent school sector now has a more diverse ethnic mix than the state school sector in the UK.

For the international children themselves, the advantages of the UK independent schools are manifold. They receive an exceptional level of education, which will qualify them for university entrance anywhere in the world. Those who come to the rural boarding schools will also enjoy the benefits of a life in the idyllic environment of the English countryside, with like-minded British and international children and a stimulating program of activities. For children of highly mobile international families, their boarding school may sometimes be the one constant in their lives, a mainstay of their educational and emotional development.

Having such a large proportion of international pupils in a school brings a variety of benefits to the schools themselves. On the practical level, these children often come from wealthy families with high expectations of the facilities and amenities, so the competition for these pupils has resulted in a general improvement in boarding accommodation. The more fundamental benefits are felt in the academic and social environment. With a diverse student population, the educational environment of a school itself becomes international. Academically, international students add a breadth of experience in the classroom which is invaluable in subjects such as History and Religious Studies. In language studies, the advantage of having bi-, tri- and quadrilingual children in a school is self-evident. The cosmopolitan classroom prepares its pupils for life on a global stage. And socially, the entire student cohort benefits from the cross-cultural friendships formed in these schools.

The upshot of all this is that international children are warmly welcomed at many an independent school in the UK and most schools will do everything within their power to accommodate these children and their parents. The influx of international families has contributed to a greater flexibility in admissions procedures of the schools in general. The dedicated international schools in the cities tend not to pursue the formal 11+ and 13+ entry procedures outlined in these pages, but have a rolling admissions program, with individualised testing in the major subjects. The city independents, too, may accommodate a strong international applicant by way of exam procedures that differ from those for local applicants. International applicants should be aware, however, that these schools are often heavily oversubscribed by local applicants and hence that their child will be competing against a very strong local field.

The greater number of openings for international students will naturally be in the boarding schools. It is here that the schools may do the most to try to accommodate international candidates. They may, for example, set exams that do not presume English as a first language. They may conduct a private tour at a time that is convenient to the parents, rather than expect parents to be present at open days. This flexibility will continue once the child is a pupil at the school: the school may, for example, rearrange the child's curriculum so as to concentrate more heavily on certain subjects. Parent/teacher exchanges may be conducted by phone, at a time that recognises time zone differences, rather than at the usual evening meetings. In many schools, the system of 'exeat' weekends (weekends where boarders return home) has effectively been scrapped, as children take their weekends away as and when it is possible for them to do so. While many children go home on the weekends, the boarding houses will organise special activities for children who remain: visits to cinemas, funfairs and the like.

Parents applying from overseas most commonly apply for a place at a boarding house, so the questions to do with boarding house visits in Chapter Two are pertinent. Some issues in particular deserve highlighting. It is a good idea, for example, to establish early in your investigations how many children in a boarding house standardly remain over the weekend and how many remain in the boarding house during the course of an entire term. It would be better to choose a school with a solid commitment to its boarding children, rather than a school that empties out over the weekend, leaving those few who are left feeling abandoned. Similarly, you might try to establish the percentage of parents who regularly attend functions at the school. While there is no obligation on parents to be present at any particular event, your child may still feel neglected if every other child in the boarding house has a visit from parents every other week. Some international children will not be concerned by this, of course, and the situation of these children is much improved of late by the advent of Skype and other programs which make communication easier.

International parents may wish to pay close attention to the qualifications the schools offer and consider whether the International Baccalaureate may offer a qualification that is more widely recognised internationally than the more common A-levels. Parents should also consider the numbers of international students in the boarding house, and ask about the support these children are given to help orientate them to British culture. Parents should expect a school with a reasonable international cohort to have a dedicated staff member in charge of international students, who can offer advice on such matters as visas, travel, and so on.

Parents applying from overseas should ask in particular about the school's policy on the role of a UK-based guardian. Some schools require the name and address of one or more guardians, who will be readily available to discuss with staff any problems that may arise with the child. Some schools also require that the guardian be responsible for the child were he or she to become unwell. These schools may be unlikely to offer a place to a child were his or her guardianship arrangements deemed unsatisfactory. If your child is coming from overseas and you do not have a guardian who can perform this role for you, you should contact an advisory service or one of the companies that will help locate a suitable guardian. There is an association by the name of AEGIS (Association for the Education and Guardianship of International Students) whose website has listings of such companies.

The last issue that must be raised is language. A huge percentage of children in the independent sector today speak another language besides English - and often two or three other languages. This can be a huge advantage to these children and also, of course, to others in the school who study the language. Having a second language, particularly a modern European or a major world language, is often an advantage in an application for a UK independent school. Parents with a child for whom English is a second language should nevertheless bear in mind that, with the exception of the consulate and other bilingual schools, the medium of tuition in the independent schools is English. Classes in most schools are fast-paced and children are expected to be able to keep up.

The level of English required to excel in the public examinations is very high. It is not normally possible to sit GSCE in these schools without sitting several subjects in the humanities - at the very least, English language

THE 11+ AND 13+ HANDBOOK

and English literature - where fluency in the language is an absolute prerequisite. The public exams are marked competitively and your child's competition will of course be native English speakers. The school will be able to advise you about the level of English they expect on entry, but it will need to be at a reasonable level at either 11+ or 13+ if your child is to attain the expected grades in these subjects. The school may stipulate that the child must have been taught in the medium of English for a certain number of years prior to entering the school. If your child is not fully fluent in English, this may be further reason to prefer a boarding school, where your child will have the greatest opportunity to improve his or her language skills and also the support with homework that may be needed.

THE 11+ AND 13+ HANDBOOK

CHAPTER NINE
BURSARY APPLICATIONS

i. Should I apply for a bursary?

The Independent Schools Council reports that over one third of the student body in its member schools is receiving help with fees of one kind or another. This support may come from the schools themselves, from the school's charitable foundations, or from the sizeable number of charitable trusts established in the UK to target children's welfare. They also point out that this number is growing, year on year, as the schools work harder to top up their bursary funds, whether by seeking direct sponsorships or by diverting funds formerly allocated to other projects into the bursary funds. For example, in recent years, many schools have appropriated scholarship moneys for their bursary funds, so that they may be directed to families in the greatest need. Some of the independent schools are dispersing millions of pounds a year from these bursary funds and offering dozens of places to children, with up to 100% fee remission.

The message voiced by the Heads of the independent schools - very loudly and clearly - is that parents should not be embarrassed to say that they may be in need of financial help to pursue the education they want for their child. Here are their reasons:

- First, the Registrars and Bursars are keenly aware that their schools are expensive and prohibitively so for many families. Admitting financial need in the face of so huge a financial challenge is not something that one should feel embarrassed about.

- Second, the Registrars and Bursars at these schools receive questions about financial support and requests from those seeking financial support so commonly that there is nothing you can ask that has not been asked many times before.

- Third, giving financial aid to families is part of the remit of the schools and of the jobs of those to whom you will speak about bursaries. Most schools have bursary funds - some of which go back into medieval times - which must be dispersed. They are actively trying to find families to act as their recipients. For both the schools and their Bursars, matching bursaries to families is not a matter of charity, but simply part of their work.

123

THE 11+ AND 13+ HANDBOOK

- Fourth, by pursuing a bursary application, the parents show that they care enough about their child's education to 'bear their financial souls' to these schools. Everyone recognises that asking for financial help is not easy. The Heads and the governing bodies of these schools wish to know that the bursaries are going to children whose parents appreciate that it is worth the effort.

If you wish to apply for a bursary at an independent school, the most important piece of information you need is this: each school and institution will conduct its process of bursary dispersal using its own systems and criteria, which will likely be different from those of others. You will have to go about the entire process with a military zeal. It will take a great deal of effort to establish the different criteria employed by the different schools and other institutions. Some of the information will be on the websites of the schools themselves, but some must be obtained from the Registrars and Bursars. It will also take effort to provide these schools and institutions with all the information they need to assess your application.

In particular, there may be differences across the schools in the income thresholds of bursary holders. Many schools do not give a figure from the outset about the income of successful bursary applicants. As a rough guide, if you are applying for a bursary at one of the London schools, and your combined family income is less than £20,000 or thereabouts, a bursary might cover the full cost of the fees, whereas if your combined income is over £45,000-50,000, you will not qualify. At some schools, the cut-off may be higher - up to £60-70,000 - but this is unusual. The following, published by the Girls' Day School Trust (a group of 26 independent girls' day schools) is representative:

Most higher-value bursaries are awarded to pupils from families with a total income of less than £19,500 per year who have no capital assets other than their home. It is highly unlikely that a bursary would be awarded to a family whose annual income is greater than £40,000 (or £45,000 for London schools), other than in very exceptional circumstances.

If you are resident in the countryside, the income thresholds will normally be lower. Schools differ in terms of both the funds available and in terms of the criteria used to select bursary holders, so it is worth checking in advance with the particular schools you are interested in.

If you wish to apply for a bursary at an independent school, you should be aware that the school will look at your financial position very closely: your income, your mortgage, the cars you drive, the holidays you take. Some people will find it intrusive. The Bursar will want to assess not merely your income, but also your assets. The schools will want to know that an offer of a bursary goes to those whose need is greatest. The bursary fund will of course have a limit, so you will be competing against others. For example, if you are a small family and own a large family house with excess bedrooms, then you may be judged less needy than another family who rent a small apartment. Equally, if you are a two-parent family with only one parent working, the school may wish to know your plans for the other parent to gain employment. You should bear in mind that many families drive their finances into the ground to afford independent school fees and it is certainly not unknown for families to sell or remortgage the family home to do so. If merely in fairness to such families, the Bursars wish to know that your need is genuine. The admissions staff may make a visit to your home, to ensure that your situation is as you have represented it.

The further thing to bear in mind is that the cost of going to an independent school is not limited to the school fees themselves. There will also be charges for uniforms, trips, music equipment, music lessons, sports equipment, sports tours, books, laptops, stationary, exams and so on. The rule of thumb is to add another ten per cent on top of the school fees to allow for these extra expenses. These extra expenses will be patchy: in some school terms, there will be few extra expenses, while others will be more expensive. These extra expenses should be taken into consideration in your bursary application.

The last preliminary point is that the school will consider your child, in the first instance, independent of your financial position. Any school considering your child will first want to establish that the school is a good 'fit' for your child. Only once the school is convinced that your child fits the profile will it consider your eligibility for a bursary. Thus the school will focus on your child's academic, musical, sporting or other skills and abilities, first and foremost. You should take the school's lead: this is what you too should focus on, if you wish to be successful in gaining a bursary at an independent school.

ii.   What bursaries are available?

The greatest difficulty for bursary applicants is that it requires a great deal of effort to establish which bursaries are available. Generally speaking, the best place to start is by asking for information from the schools themselves. The Bursars and the Admission Staff will be able to give you the details of how bursaries are administered in their school and will be able to advise whether you may fit the criteria. The staff may also know about other sources of funding that may be available to you and may be able to approach funding bodies with your child in mind.

Many of the schools with large charitable foundations in the UK are very old. Some of the foundations themselves go back to medieval times. (If you read, for example, about a 'Queen's Scholarship' fund set up by Queen Elizabeth, do not assume that it is Queen Elizabeth II who is responsible.) At that time, these 'public' schools were of course for boys only. (The Queen's Scholarships were originally for 'the sons of decay'd gentlemen.') Many of these schools have remained single sex. It has been suggested that, as a result, total bursary funds across the UK skew towards male recipients. Whether or not this is the case, there are a great number of scholarships at the old 'public' schools that provide the path not only to a place in the school itself, but also to a bursary.

How good are your child's chances of winning one of these bursaries? Whether boy or girl, your child will in general stand a greater chance of gaining a bursary if he or she has proven abilities or achievements. Many schools award scholarships on the basis of academic, sporting and artistic achievement. Many schools award bursaries to the scholarship recipients before others. For these schools, the aim of gaining a bursary will thus be secondary to the prior aim of gaining a scholarship, since the bursary will be, in effect, a paid scholarship. (Look at the section on scholarships in Chapter One for more.) Even for those schools which do not prioritise scholarship winners, evidence that a child will help the school's attainment in public exams or evidence that a child can make a specific contribution to a schools' orchestra or fencing team, for example, will not be overlooked. Also, a previous connection to the school would in all probability be helpful to a bursary application.

Further to this, if your child has specific skills in the creative arts - in music, voice or dance - there may be funded positions at specialised independent schools available to you. These include the UK's many choir schools. The Choir School Association reports: 'Chorister places are generously subsidised thanks to the cathedral, collegiate and choir school foundations. The CSA administers the Government's Choir School Scholarship Scheme which can provide additional funds following strict means-testing.' Along related lines, the Department of Education's Music and Dance Scheme offers places at a number of independent specialist schools: 'The MDS is a small and highly-specialised scheme that provides means-tested fee support and grants to designated centres of excellence for the education and vocational training of exceptionally talented young musicians and dancers.'

Other scholarships are more specific again: if a member of your family belongs to a certain profession, there may be bursaries available from the livery company associated with that profession. There are specific bursaries available to the children of clergy, those of seafarers, those who have worked in the City of London and, at Sixth Form, to future members of the Armed Services. The Charities Commission keeps details of all charities providing such bursaries. Also, the Educational Trusts Forum gives information of 25 registered charities that administer grants and awards to assist families in need who cannot afford educational or boarding fees.

If a child's situation is one of very great need, his or her situation will be considered very seriously, both by the schools themselves and by charities set up specifically for vulnerable children. In such cases, the child's academic ability may play a less prominent role in considerations than his or her immediate needs. Such children might include: children with parents whose work or other commitments makes it impossible to provide stable parenting; children with parents who are incapacitated, ill or for other reasons incapable of stable parenting; children whose siblings are incapacitated and require intensive parenting; children cared for by grandparents, other family members, foster parents or other guardians.

There are a number of institutions in the UK set up specifically to support these children's education. The Buttle Trust is one: 'The young people we help have significant health, emotional, social or family difficulties. By meeting their needs through a supportive and stable secondary education we aim to give them the best possible opportunity to thrive.' Likewise the Springboard Foundation, whose 'objective is to add a powerful, ambitious and innovative approach to the provision of fully funded bursary places at independent and state boarding schools for disadvantaged children.' And again, the Royal National Children's Foundation 'helps vulnerable children and young people in Britain whose circumstances are seriously prejudicial to their normal development and where no other care is available.'

The quotes in this section come from the websites of the associations, foundations and trusts themselves. These are listed in the Independent Junction website, with links. Those doing detailed research on available bursaries should look at this website for an extensive list of useful websites. One last point to note: bursaries are usually reserved for British citizens. If you have a child in an independent school and are not a citizen, and your circumstances change during the course of your child's attendance in the school, the school may look upon a bursary request favourably. The school would in all likelihood want to have reason to keep the child at the school, in terms of the contribution that it believes the child is making.

THE 11+ AND 13+ HANDBOOK

iii. Tips for bursary applicants

If you intend to apply for a bursary for your child to complete an independent school education, there are a number of things to bear in mind:

- The advice given by schools is to make it clear from the outset that you are thinking of applying for a bursary, so that you will be able to get the best advice from the school at an early stage, rather than raising hopes that may not be realistic. The Admissions Staff will be able to help you by outlining the general criteria that need to be met and discuss your particular circumstances in detail.

- Each school or institution has its own criteria for the award of bursaries. The general advice given by the Bursars is that successful bursary candidates tend to fit these criteria fairly precisely. Thus, it is not worth trying to fit yourselves into categories that will not fit. It is better to spend your time on applications with some prospect of success.

- It is not possible to determine in the abstract whether you will be eligible for a bursary. There is no abstract metric that is used by the schools to determine when a family is in need of financial help. Each application is considered on its merits. This is why it is worth speaking to the Bursar early in the application process to discuss your situation.

- The school may consider the situation of your family as a whole. The school will look at the specific needs of the child and the benefit he or she will gain from what the school can offer. But it may also look at the needs of other members of the family as well and the benefit to them of the child attending the school. So, for example, if the child has a younger sibling with special needs, it may be beneficial to *both* siblings if the older child boards, in that it frees the mother to care for the child with special needs at home.

- Many schools may be persuaded by a genuine attempt to contribute some portion of the fees on the part of a bursary recipient. Many independent school children receive help from grandparents and other relatives. You may wish to inquire whether this is possible for your child as well.

- You may stand a better chance of receiving a bursary if you can

128

contribute some percentage of the fees yourself. Bursaries covering a percentage of the school fees are generally more common than full-fee bursaries.

- Most bursaries are reassessed annually. If your circumstances change for the better, your bursary may be withdrawn. Equally, if you have a place at a school and your circumstances change for the worse, you may be able to secure a bursary ahead of others. You may be wish to ask the school whether it can ensure that the bursary level will remain stable during the course of your child's school career, assuming that your income remains stable.

- It is best to get started early in your search for suitable schools. Some children receive a bursary from prep school onwards. Indeed, a child who is successful in a prep school will have the support of the prep school Head, when making an application for a bursary at a senior school. This may be a great advantage.

- Some schools waive the registration fee for bursary applicants. Find out whether this is so for the schools for which you are registering.

- Those seeking a bursary should try to avoid merely opting for the best offer financially. The primary consideration will be whether the child is suited to the school that makes the offer, rather than the offer itself. You may be better-advised to prefer an offer which is less financially lucrative at a school where you are confident that the child will be successful.

- The award of a bursary will be subject to your child's success at the school. The bursaries information published by the Girls' Day School Trust, for example, includes a note that a bursary may be withdrawn if a bursary recipients 'behaviour or work is unsatisfactory'. This would likely be rare, but the thinking here is that a school's bursary funds ought go to a deserving recipient.

- You are strongly advised to inform the school if you wish to be considered for a place even if you are not successful in gaining a bursary. Some schools, it appears, tend not to make offers to bursary applicants should their bursary application be unsuccessful. (This is of course difficult; the school will naturally wish to know how you plan to pay its fees, in the absence of a bursary.)

CHAPTER TEN
RESOURCES

i. Resources for school searches

The list of websites explicitly mentioned in past chapters may be found at the back of this book. So as to keep information up-to-date and to expand the listings as new information comes online or on hand, the most recent lists of resources are maintained at the website linked to this book: www.IndependentJunction.co.uk. There you will find links to the websites listed, along with lists of websites and other resources in the following categories:

- websites for conducting school searches, such as the websites of the Independent Schools Council, the Scottish Council of Independent Schools, the Headmasters' and Headmistresses' Conference and other independent companies such as Independent Schools of the British Isles (ibsi), *The Good Schools Guide* and best-schools.co.uk;

- websites for finding school inspection reports provided by the Independent Schools Commission, OFSTED and other school inspectorates;

- school league tables, such as those of *The Telegraph*, *The Independent* and *The Sunday Times* newspapers, the BBC and best-schools.co.uk;

- magazines and newspapers that focus on independent schools, such as the *Tatler Schools Guide*, *The Spectator Guide to Independent Schools* and *The Sunday Times* 'Parent Power';

- other places to go for information relevant to the 11+ and 13+ admissions processes, such as forums, school shows and so on;

- exam preparation materials and websites with preparation materials in each subject, especially the free specimen papers provided by some of the independent schools for their applicants;

- information about universities, such as the website of UCAS and the Russell Group universities;

- information for children with Special Educational Needs, such as The

Council for the Registration of Schools Teaching Dyslexic Pupils, IPSEA, British Dyslexia Association, Dyslexia Action and the Dyspraxia Foundation;

- information about boarding schools, such as *The Metropolis UK Boarding Schools Guide*, and ukboardingschools.com;

- information about a large number of associations, trusts, foundations and organisations that provide bursaries to independent schools, too many to mention;

- private consultancies and tutoring agencies that provide guidance on independent school admissions and exam preparation;

- information for international parents, such as agencies that provide guardians for their children.

If you are in the process of applying for independent schools, these websites - in addition to the websites of the schools themselves - should provide you with most of what you need to know. If however, you have further questions - such as questions about the admissions procedures at particular schools - you can post them on the appropriate forum on that website. Parents who have been through the process of 11+ and 13+ are very warmly invited to share their information and experience on these forums.

ii. Resources for exam preparation

Besides time, space and a good deal of patience, the most important thing required for the 11+ and 13+ exams and pretests is a good set of preparation materials. What sort of materials should these be? The answer will of course depend on the specific exams your child will sit. You will need to know two things about these exams: first, the subjects to be examined and, second, the form of the exams. Information about the first will be available on the school's website; information about second may be more difficult to obtain. Some schools publish specimen papers, which may be available from the school's website or may be sent to you after you register. Even if a school does not publish such papers, the papers of other comparable schools are a useful guide to the general format of these exams.

Once you know (as best as possible) what is involved in these exams, use this information to construct an achievable preparation schedule. Make a

THE 11+ AND 13+ HANDBOOK

list of the areas for which preparation is needed, prioritising those areas where your child is weakest. If your child is especially weak in spelling or grammar, for example, you should try to find ten minutes to concentrate on them every day. If your child will be examined in Verbal Reasoning, and has never come across a VR exercise before, it may require several sessions per week for a period of some weeks to become familiar with them.

Then, make a list of resources available in each subject. Make the list as varied as possible. Use a variety of media: use online as well as paper resources, for example. Think of ways to make the work more enjoyable. Include games and puzzles in your preparation for the Maths exam, for example. Such resources can be found online at a number of websites: primaryresources.co.uk is a good place to start. The range of these materials you use will depend on how much time you have - that is, whether you are starting your exam preparation one year or one month in advance of the exams.

If you have very little time for preparation, skip most other things and go straight to specimen exams in Maths and English and practice papers in Reasoning (if this is being examined), adding a few mental maths, spelling, grammar and punctuation exercises for variety. The specimen exams are the best preparation for the actual exams, not merely in terms of subject matter, but also in terms of practice at building attention span and exam technique. If you have only a few weeks, the variation in your program must be provided by the range of subjects you cover each night. Try to cover at least two subjects, making the activities as varied as possible.

Here is an example of what your schedule might look like if you are starting last-minute, with merely weeks to go before the exams:

Monday	a spelling test (10 mins), a Maths exam (50 mins)
Tuesday	a grammar exercise (10 mins), a Reasoning paper (20 mins), a comprehension paper (30 mins)
Wednesday	a mental maths exercise (10 mins), a Reasoning paper (20 mins), a creative writing piece (30 mins)
Thursday	a spelling test (10 mins), a grammar exercise (10 mins), two Maths papers (40 mins)
Friday	a mental maths exercise (10 mins), a Reasoning paper (20 mins), a comprehension paper (30 mins)
Saturday	a Maths exam (60 mins), an English exam (60 mins)

This is intensive; it is the sort of regime suggested for those coming to exam preparation late. Remember that a few minutes must be allocated at

132

THE 11+ AND 13+ HANDBOOK

the beginning of each session for going over mistakes from the previous session and a few minutes must be allocated at the end for reinforcing what has been learnt. And remember that your child's school work takes precedence. If your child is being given a copious amount of homework from his or her school, this plan may not be achievable.

If you have more time for preparation, you can afford to be more relaxed, both in terms of the amount of time you spend each day and in terms of what is included as exam preparation. Work through a few of the specimen exams, to give you and your child an idea of what the exams will look like, and then use them sparingly - one or two a week - leaving the majority for the weeks prior to the exams. Instead, use shorter practice papers and online materials. If you are starting well ahead of the exams, your program might look something like this:

Monday	a mental maths exercise (10 mins), a Reasoning paper (20 mins)
Tuesday	a grammar exercise (10 mins), some online maths exercises or a maths practice paper (20 mins)
Wednesday	a comprehension paper (30 mins)
Thursday	a creative writing piece (30 mins)
Friday	a spelling test (10 mins), a Reasoning paper (20 mins)
Saturday	a Maths specimen exam (60 mins)

Once you have a preparation schedule in place, you will have a better idea of the range and extent of the materials you will require: so many specimen exams in Maths and English, so many practice papers in Maths, English and Reasoning, exercises for mental maths, for grammar and for punctuation, and word lists for spelling tests. For the specimen exams, go to the Independent Junction website, where you will find a list of about 250 such exams, available from the websites of the independent schools themselves. Some other free Maths, English and Reasoning papers can also be found from this website.

For the Maths, English and Reasoning practice papers, it is best to go to a bookshop with a large educational book section and look through the full range of materials available. You will have no trouble locating them; there is a huge demand for these materials and at least a dozen publishers producing new materials each year. It will take some time to compare the materials and find the ones that appeal to you. Look below in the subject listings for suggestions, and for other ideas of materials that could provide variation in your preparation program.

133

THE 11+ AND 13+ HANDBOOK

[One thing to note when you search for '11+ resources' in bookshops or online: be careful to avoid materials intended for the grammar school market. These materials are typically multiple choice or use a format that can be machine-read. The Reasoning papers work well enough for both grammar and independent markets (though even there, there are differences: the independent exams tend to be less formulaic and more generic than the grammar). However, the 'Introduction to the 11+' books presently on the market, the '11+ mock exams' and various other '11+ survival guides' are all intended either solely or primarily for grammar school applicants. There are also several '11+' websites geared to the grammar school market.]

a. English

- In English, the best preparation for the independent school exams will be the English specimen exam papers published by the independent schools themselves, a great number of which are listed on the Independent Junction website. These are particularly good for mock exams, prior to the exams. These specimen exams typically do not include answers, so you will have to mark them yourself, but they may include the marks allocated to each question, which is useful for practising how to allocate your time. Use your own judgement as regards marking, remembering that the aim is for clear and concise sentences, with a point made for every mark earned. You do not need to be too strict in your marking: the precise mark attained is less important than the practice these papers provide.

- Beyond these, the best preparation is reading short texts and discussing them together. Look at the specimen papers to get an idea of the types of question asked in a comprehension piece. You can easily find texts that will interest your child: short passages of about 800-1200 words in length. The following are good: short articles in magazines or newspapers; sections from your child's favourite books; sections from books your child has not read; sections of children's textbooks in history, science, the arts or other interests of your child. Go to the children's section of the library together and let your child pick out a range of books for these exercises.

- There are a number of books of comprehension papers on the market. The most popular publishers are Bonds, GCP, Letts and Schofield & Sims. Look at the reviews on Amazon of the particular books that interest you. The reviewers are often using them for 11+ and 13+

preparation themselves and will give advice about the books' academic level. If you are working towards a highly selective school, work towards books at a higher level than those set for your child's age.

- ISEB offers specimen exams in English on their website and publishes its past papers for both 11+ and 13+ exams, available from the Galore Park website. Even if your child is not sitting the Common Entrance exams set by ISEB, these materials will be set at the right level. These papers may be used for your school's mock exams, so check with the teacher before giving them to your child.

- For variation, 11+ children can try the past SATs papers at Key Stage 2 (KS2) at Level 5 and Level 6 (which is the highest level for KS2). These are the papers students sit across the UK for the National Curriculum assessments at the end of Year 6. In English, they are not in the same format as the independent school exams, but may provide a welcome change of format.

- For the comprehension exam, another useful resource is a list of the English vocabulary your child can use: alliteration, assonance, metaphor, simile, etc. There is a list of such vocabulary on the Independent Junction website and you will also find such lists in some of the books of English practice papers. Test your child on these terms repeatedly, so that your child feels confident to use them.

- A full English preparation program might also include daily spelling tests and exercises in grammar and punctuation. Some independent schools test these in dedicated exams or sections of their exams. Even if not, they will be tested in the written composition paper. You will find many exercise books in grammar and punctuation at the bookshop or online. For spelling lists, the *Complete Graded Spelling Lists for Years One to Six* (available from Amazon) is the most comprehensive.

- There are also online materials that can be used for practice in English spelling, punctuation and grammar: try the BBC's Bitesize website (though the levels are not challenging; try a level higher than that for your child's age group). A word of warning about online materials in English: avoid the American sites, because of the problem of the spelling. There are sufficient materials for you to use without having to resort to American resources.

THE 11+ AND 13+ HANDBOOK

- For the written composition exam, take the questions on the specimen exam papers as your guide on topics. You can find a list of typical questions on the Independent Junction website, along with further advice for preparing for the composition piece. You cannot grade your child's composition papers, but you can check spelling, punctuation, grammar and paragraph structure. Remember that the topic of the composition and the length of the piece are of less importance than the way in which the composition is crafted. You can help your child by discussing a range of possible responses to each question, contrasting the different ways a question might be approached. The best help may be merely to encourage your child to use his or her imagination.

- For those with more time available, a preparation for English could include Scrabble, crosswords, word searches and other word games. Look online or look in a good bookshop for books of these.

b. Mathematics

- In Mathematics, the specimen exam papers of the schools themselves are again the best preparation. In Maths, unlike English and Reasoning, these exams can be used more than once. After a few weeks or so, you can repeat an exam so as to reinforce what the child has learnt when they worked through the questions the first time and to tackle once again any questions they found difficult. There are a great number of these exams listed on the Independent Junction website. A few provide answers and some show the marks per question, which is useful for practising how to allocate your time. If you mark these papers together with your child, you will reinforce what he or she has learnt.

- The exercise books and practice papers available from the bookshop are also good for quick practice sessions, since they are often about twenty minutes in length and also give answers. The most well-established publishers are Bonds and CGP. The exercises in these books tend to be rather simpler than the more complex questions towards the end of the independent school exams. You can compensate for this to some extent by working at a higher level than the books set for your child's age. These exercise books will nevertheless help with the arithmetic. Look for books with questions that are 'worded' rather than merely numerical.

136

THE 11+ AND 13+ HANDBOOK

- You will find these more complex problem-solving questions in the past papers of the UK Mathematics Trust 'Junior Challenge', The Mathematical Association's 'Primary Maths Challenge' and The Scottish Mathematical Council's 'Mathematical Challenge'. The papers of the European 'Kangaroo Challenge', which is similar, can also be found on UK Mathematics Trust website.

- ISEB offers specimen exams in Maths on their website and publishes its past papers for both 11+ and 13+ exams, available from the Galore Park website. Even if your child is not sitting the Common Entrance exams set by ISEB, these materials will be set at the right level. These papers may be used for your school's mock exams, so check with the teacher before giving them to your child.

- 11+ children can try the past SATs papers at Key Stage 2 (KS2) at Level 5 and Level 6 (which is the highest level set for KS2). These are the papers students sit across the UK for the National Curriculum assessments at the end of Year 6. In Maths, these exams are not dissimilar in format to the independent school exams, in that a good percentage of the questions are 'worded' rather than purely numerical.

- There are some good online educational testing materials in Maths. The BBC's Bitesize series is good for basic practice in Maths, though generally not very challenging. The University of Cambridge's NRICH website has a good range of problem-solving exercises for children of all ages, so you can work at your chosen level. There are also several subscription-based maths websites, which some children may enjoy: Mathletics, MyMaths and themathsfactor.

- These can be supplemented by mental maths exercises, to get your child's 'maths brain' working more efficiently. Mental maths exercise books can be found in bookshops or online. Schofield & Sims produce some which appear to be popular. Those with more time before the exams could try other maths games, such as Soduku, for fun. There are a great number of sites with various forms of maths puzzle online: one such is Mathsphere.

- The last resource that is advised for Maths preparation is a list of the Maths vocabulary: the names of shapes, operations, angles and so on. There is a list available at the Independent Junction website, and you will find them at the back of the books of practice papers. Test your child on these terms repeatedly.

c. Verbal and Non-verbal Reasoning

- For the Reasoning exams, focus your preparation on the specific type of Reasoning in your child's exams: Verbal Reasoning (VR) or Non-verbal Reasoning (NVR). There are many books on both of these available in the bookshops and online (primarily because Reasoning is also tested in the grammar school 11+ exams). Of the many different publishing companies, Bonds, CGP and Susan Doughtrey appear to be the most popular, the latter being considered the most difficult.

- If you are starting out in either VR or NVR, look for a 'How to ...' book; there are several available, but those by Peter Williams are particularly good. Once again, the Reasoning questions set for the top independent schools tend to be at the higher end of the spectrum in difficulty. The books in VR and NVR are standardly graded from beginners to advanced levels; for the more selective independent schools, you will want to work towards the higher level. Where these books are graded by age, work towards a level higher than those set for your child's age group.

- For VR, look for the books with the broadest range of questions. Avoid the books with multiple choice answers; the questions in the independent school exams are what is called 'standard' format. You do not need to be worried about the numbering conventions of the different types of VR exercise, but simply be aware of the full range of types of question that may be asked. Use a range of publications, to give yourself the greatest variety of styles and content.

- The NVR exercises tend to be more standardised in form and so the difference between the books produced by the various publishers is not so great. Again, use books from a range of publishers, for maximum variety.

- The Independent Junction website has a comprehensive list of types of VR question and a list of vocabulary that is useful for VR exams. On this website, you will also find lists of other free material in VR and NVR available online. For example, there is a range of free online exercises at the website of one of the publishers of these Reasoning books, Athay Educational.

In short, the program of exam preparation for 11+ and 13+ exams and pretests is relatively straightforward: get together a collection of materials in the subjects your child will be examined on and work through them systematically. A supportive and well-organised adult is needed to plan, to set and mark papers, and to offer encouragement, but a tutor is not needed for this program.

Let your child take a role in setting the materials for exam preparation, deciding on the program and charting his or her success. Take your child to the bookshop and look at the exercise books and discuss which books look best and why. Choose the ones you can both agree on. Set your child the task of finding websites with good practice materials. Let your child put together the program and cross the work off as it is done. Some children will enjoy making charts and decorating them with stamps and stickers. Others will enjoy making spreadsheets and ticking off boxes. Let your child invent ways to make the process more interesting and fun.

Most important of all is to talk with your child to keep track of how they feel they are progressing. Give your child a say in how they will work through their preparation materials. Give your child a say in deciding when they have done enough on a given topic and can move on. Their judgement of whether they feel confident about that topic will probably be reliable. And, while it is best to try to stick to the program you have made, be flexible. If your child truly cannot face another comprehension passage or Verbal Reasoning exercise or whatever, by all means do something else for a change.

CONCLUSION

The 11+ and 13+ processes are probably more complicated and taxing than they ought to be. The results are worth it, however. The vast majority of children in the independent sector are happy with their senior schools. Looking back on the 11+ and 13+, many parents admit that they were overly concerned about their child's prospects. There are many excellent schools in the UK. The truth is that there are other schools that would probably work as well for your child as the one you eventually choose.

While you are going through the 11+ or 13+ admissions process, you may wish to bear in mind that any decision you make about a senior school is not binding on later years. If for some reason the school you choose does not work for your child, you can always change. Every year, there will be several children leaving each year group in a senior school and being replaced by others. (This is especially so in schools with international pupils.) At this later stage, moving from one independent school to another is usually not as difficult as the 11+ or 13+ processes. It may involve as little an interview and a reference from your present school.

It is also important to keep in mind that educational success is not merely about A-level results and university entrances. These are of course the metrics used to measure a school's success, but you will be measuring your child's success more broadly. The deeper effects of a good education have to do with strength of character: developing self-confidence, determination and resilience; building high aspirations and ambitions; learning to use a true moral compass; exploiting your imaginative and creative abilities to the fullest. Finding a school that helps your child to do this will be one of your greatest contributions to his or her education. Another will of course be helping your child gain entry to it.

Many parents put a great deal of effort into working out how to give their child a 'competitive edge' over others and so help them gain entrance to their school of choice. The best thing you can do to give your child a competitive edge is to become fully engaged in the admissions process. Most parents recognise that these examinations are difficult. Most let their child know how pleased and proud they will be when he or she does well and gains entry to their chosen school. These are not the children with the competitive edge, however. The children with the competitive edge are the children whose parents treat it as a shared experience. They are the children who will actually *enjoy* this experience because they know they will be supported at each step - from the day they first enter a senior school on tour to the day they finally enter their school in full uniform.

GLOSSARY

Boarding school - any school, independent or state, where pupils live residentially during the school term, by contrast with a day school, where children live off-site. Boarding may be offered on several different models: full boarding, where a child remains at the school throughout the school term; weekly boarding, where a pupil remains at the school during the week but returns home on the weekend; or flexi-boarding, where a more flexible arrangement is agreed between the school and parents.

Bursary - a reduction in school fees, usually awarded on the basis of financial need. Bursaries may cover these fees in their entirety or in part.

Common Entrance - a set of exams, offered by many prep schools in the independent school sector, which test children for entrance into UK independent schools at 11+ or at 13+. It was formerly offered only at 13+, so the term is used primarily for the 13+ exams and the program of study leading up to them. The Common Entrance curriculum and exams are set by the Independent Schools Examination Board (ISEB).

Day school - any school where pupils attend the school during the day only, in contrast to a boarding school, where children reside in houses at or near the school. A school may be day, boarding or both.

Department for Education (DfE) - a department of the UK government responsible for education and protection of children up to the age of 19 in England. The Department has devolved counterparts in Scotland, Wales and Northern Ireland.

Extra-curricular activities - activities which take place outside the normal schedule of classes. These activities are designed to encourage non-academic skills of an artistic, creative, sporting or social nature. They are usually selected by pupils according to their own individual interests and abilities.

Grammar school - one of 164 selective state-funded schools in England and Northern Ireland. These schools by tradition have taught an academic curriculum to the most academically gifted pupils in the state sector. Admission is based either wholly or in part on results of an 11+ examination, which is highly competitive.

Head - the Headmaster or Headmistress of a school; the person appointed by the governing body to be in charge of a school.

Independent school - a school that does not receive funding from either national or local government authorities, but is funded primarily by the school fees of its pupils.

ISC - the Independent Schools Council a non-profit organisation that represents over 1,200 independent schools, with over 500,000 pupils. It is comprised of a number of independent school associations - including the Headmasters' and Headmistresses' Conference (HMC), the Independent Association of Prep Schools (IAPS) and the Independent Schools Association (ISA) - whose aims and objectives it promotes.

ISEB - the Independent Schools Examinations Board sets curriculum and examinations for the Common Entrance examinations at 11+ and 13+. It is an independent board of prep school and senior school Heads.

ISI - the Independent Schools Inspectorate is an organisation responsible for the inspection of independent schools in England which are members of the organisations of the Independent Schools Council (ISC). Through an agreement with the Department for Education, it is empowered to carry out inspections and produce reports on each school, which are available on its website.

Public school - a term used to refer to a sub-group of UK independent schools: the older, more exclusive of the schools, which traditionally educated boys of ages 13-18 in a boarding house setting. The term is now used more widely of schools whose Heads belong to the Headmasters' and Headmistresses' Conference (HMC). The term contrasts, not with 'private schools', as in some other countries, but rather with 'prep schools', which conduct the preparatory schooling.

THE 11+ AND 13+ HANDBOOK

Prep (Preparatory) school - an independent school, traditionally educating children of ages 8-13 in preparation for entry into public schools. Now the term is used more widely for schools educating children for entry to the independent senior schools. Many of these schools also offer a 'preprep' for children from age 3.

Primary school - a school which educates children in Years 1-6 of formal education in a UK, by contrast with a 'secondary school', which educates children in Years 7-13. In the independent sector, primary schools are commonly also referred to as 'prep' schools, the term 'primary' school' being used of state schools, but such usage is not universal.

Private school - another name often used for an independent school.

Public exams - a series of exams that most students in the UK sit during the course of their secondary schooling. The most important of these are the GCSE (General Certificate of Secondary Education) at Year 11 and the A-levels (Advanced levels) at Year 13. These exams are administered by several examination boards - including AQA, Edexcel and OCR - which are responsible for setting and awarding secondary qualifications for UK students. See 'Secondary Qualifications in UK Schools', below.

Secondary school - a school which educates children in Years 7-13 of formal education in a UK, by contrast with a 'primary school', which educates children in Years 1-6. In the independent sector, secondary schools are commonly also referred to as 'senior' schools, the term 'secondary school' being used of state schools, but such usage is not universal.

Selective school - a term primarily used for a school in the state sector which selects its pupils either wholly or in part on the basis of academic achievement or aptitude. In recent years the term has referred to grammar schools which, by contrast with comprehensive schools ('comps'), select pupils for entry at 11+ on some basis other than geographical. Some of the new academies also belong to this category.

Sixth Form - a name commonly given to the two years of study (Years 12 and 13) in which students study towards their final school exams (AS and A-level, pre-U or IB) prior to entering the tertiary sector.

State schools (also known as 'maintained schools') are funded by taxes and are free to pupils between the ages of 3 and 18 years. State schools follow the National Curriculum and set National Curriculum Tests (NCTs), which used to be called SATs and are still referred to by that name. Over 90% of children in the UK attend state schools. Within this state sector are: comprehensive schools, which select children usually on the basis of the distance of their home from the school gate; grammar schools, which select children on the basis performance at competitive 11+ exams; specialist schools, which specialise in certain subjects and select children on the basis of aptitude; faith schools, operated by religious organisations; academies and free schools, operated by educational charities; and state boarding schools, which charge for boarding (to a limit of £12,000) but not for tuition.

Scholarship - an award given to pupils, usually at the end of the admissions process, in recognition of academic, sporting, artistic, dramatic or other form of achievement. Most independent schools offer scholarships of one kind or another. Scholarships are often (but not always) attended by a reduction in school or other tuition fees, or may entitle one to be considered for a bursary.

THE 11+ AND 13+ HANDBOOK

SECONDARY QUALIFICATIONS IN THE UK

GCSE - the General Certificate of Secondary Education is an academic qualification awarded in a specified subject. Students normally sit a series of GCSE subjects (in an independent school, usually 10-12) in Years 10 and 11 of their secondary schooling. They are examined in those subjects in Year 11 (though students may sit one or two exams earlier). Students pass with a grade ranging from A* to G. Many independent schools stipulate that students must attain a certain grade at GCSE to continue with that subject at A-levels. GCSE qualifications are administered by a number of different examinations boards, including AQA, Edexcel and OCR.

IGCSE - the International General Certificate of Secondary Education (IGCSE) is a variation on the GSCE academic qualification. IGCSE subjects are taught and examined in many independent schools, being considered more rigorous in some subjects than GCSE. Many independent schools 'mix and match' GCSE and IGCSE qualifications in various subjects. IGCSE qualifications are administered by Cambridge International Examinations. (See the Cambridge International Examinations website for more information.)

A-level - the 'Advanced' level qualifications are offered by most independent senior schools in England, Wales and Northern Ireland in Years 12 and 13 as the principle university entrance qualification. A-levels consists of two parts: AS levels (which stand as a qualification in their own right) and A2 levels. Students usually take three or four of each, involving a range of exams and other testing procedures, and are awarded a pass with a grade ranging from A* to E. UK and international universities standardly base their conditional admissions offers on a student's predicted A-level grades. Many university courses stipulate required subjects and grades. A-level qualifications are administered by a number of different examinations boards, including AQA, Edexcel and OCR.

Cambridge pre-U - an alternative to the A-level qualification offered by a number of independent schools in some or all subjects taken by students in Years 12-13 and examined in Year 13. It is recognised as a university entrance qualification by top universities internationally. Students taking a full Pre-U Diploma are graded out of a possible 96 marks and receive a Pass, Merit or Distinction grade for each of three principle subjects, an Independent Research Project, and a Global Perspectives portfolio. Cambridge pre-U qualifications are administered by Cambridge International Examinations. (See the Cambridge International Examinations website for more information.)

International Baccalaureate (IB) - a diploma awarded by the International Baccalaureate Organisation (IBO), headquartered in Geneva. The IB is offered by many independent schools in the UK and abroad, and is recognised as a qualification for most universities, both in the UK and internationally. Students taking a full IB Diploma are graded out of a possible 45 marks, in six subjects (of which at least three are studied at a higher level), an extended essay, a 'Theory of Knowledge' program and a 'Creativity, action, service' (CAS) program. (See the IBO's website for more information.)

Higher and Advanced Higher (Scotland) - in the Scottish secondary education system, the Higher is one of the national school-leaving certificate exams and university entrance qualifications of the Scottish Qualifications Certificate (SQC), equivalent to the AS-level in the English system. Advanced Higher is an optional further qualification, equivalent to A2-level, normally taken after students have completed Highers, for qualification for English universities. These qualifications are administered by the Scottish Qualifications Authority (SQA).

143

WEBSITES REFERENCED IN THIS BOOK

Links to these sites and others that may be of interest can be found on the website associated with this book, Independent Junction: www.independentjunction.co.uk.

Association for the Education and Guardianship of International Students (AEGIS): aegisuk.net
Athay Educational: www.athey-educational.co.uk/menu.htm
BBC Bitesize: www.bbc.co.uk/bitesize/ks2
Best Schools: www.best-schools.co.uk
British Dyslexia Association: www.bdadyslexia.org.uk
Cambridge International Examinations: www.cie.org.uk/programmes-and-qualifications
The Council for the Registration of Schools Teaching Dyslexic Pupils (Crested): www.crested.org.uk
Department of Education Performance Tables: www.education.gov.uk/schools/performance
Dyslexia Action: dyslexiaaction.org.uk
The Dyspraxia Foundation: www.dyspraxiafoundation.org.uk
Eleven Plus Exams: www.elevenplusexams.co.uk
Galore Park: www.galorepark.co.uk
The Girls' Day School Trust (gdst): http://m.gdst.net
The Good Schools Guide: www.goodschoolsguide.co.uk
The Headmasters' and Headmistresses' Conference (HMC): www.hmc.org.uk
The Independent Schools Council (ISC): www.hmc.org.uk
Independent Schools Examinations Board (ISEB): www.iseb.co.uk
The Independent Schools Inspectorate (ISI): www.isi.net
Independent Schools of the British Isles (ibsi): www.isbi.com
The Independent Schools Show: www.schoolsshow.co.uk
International Baccalaureate Organisation (IBO) website: www.ibo.org
IPSEA: www.ipsea.org.uk
The Mathematical Association Primary Mathematics Challenge: www.m-a.org.uk/jsp/index.jsp?lnk=250
The Metropolis UK Boarding Schools Guide: www.metropolis.co.uk/business-publishing/uk-boarding-schools-guide
Mumsnet: www.Mumsnet.com
Primary resources: www.primaryresources.co.uk
Russell Group: http: www.russellgroup.ac.uk
Scottish Council of Independent Schools: http://www.scis.org.uk
Scottish Mathematical Council Mathematical Challenge: www.wpr3.co.uk/MC/
The Spectator Guide to Independent Schools: www.spectator.co.uk/the-spectator-and-education
Tatler Schools Guide: www.tatler.co.uk/guides/schools-guide/2013
UK Boarding Schools: www.ukboardingschools.com
UK Mathematics Trust Junior Challenge: www.ukmt.org.uk/individual-competitions/junior-challenge
Universities and Colleges Admission Service (UCAS): www.ucas.com
University of Cambridge NRICH: nrich.maths.org/frontpage

THE 11+ AND 13+ HANDBOOK

SCHOOL VISIT FORM

This form is available for download from the Independent Junction website: www.IndependentJunction.co.uk:

www.IndependentJunction.co.uk						School Visit Form
(This page is taken from *The 11+ and 13+ Handbook* by Victoria Barker)						
School						
Address and phone						
General information	Boys Girls Co-ed	☐ ☐ ☐	Day Boarding	☐ ☐	Number of pupils	
Name of Head						
Name of Registrar						
Date and cost of initial registration						
Notes from Initial Research						
Curriculum - A-Level/IB, languages, etc						
League Table results - GCSE, A-levels						
Admissions procedure - pre-tests and/or exams - dates						
What is distinctive about this school?						
Notes from School Visit						
Facilities, environment						
Students						
Staff						
Head						
Extra-curricular activities						
Quality of pastoral care						
Atmosphere, philosophy, ethos						
Next Actions						

ABOUT THE AUTHOR

The author is a primary school governor with many years of experience as an educationalist: she has two PhDs and has had a career teaching at university level. It was, however, as a parent that she acquired the information in these pages. The information was gathered while preparing a daughter and son for the 11+ and 13+ examinations respectively. Her approach was hands on, tutor-free, and by and large a very happy one.

She was inspired to write this book because, during the course of these admissions, she realised that she and other parents were often making crucial decisions about their children's futures on the basis of incomplete information. And after the admissions were finalised, far too many parents were commenting: 'If only I knew then what I know now, I would have done things slightly differently ...' In this book, she passes on the results of several years of research, many, many school visits and innumerable hours of discussion with Heads, Registrars, Bursars, teachers, fellow parents and forum communicants.

Printed in Great Britain
by Amazon